RURAL DEVELOPMENT: TOWARDS SUSTAINABILITY

RURAL DEVELOPMENT: TOWARDS SUSTAINABILITY

(In 3 Volumes)

(Rural Diversity and Community Development)

Volume 3

Editor

B.K. Pandey

ISHA

ISHA BOOKS

Delhi-110033

Rural Development: Towards Sustainability
(Rural Diversity and Community Development)

Rs. 2500 (Set)
Rs. 835 (Each Volume)

ISBN : 81-8205-209-2 (Set)
ISBN : 81-8205-312-9 (Vol. 3)

Published in 2005 in India by
Isha Books
D-43, Prithviraj Road.
Adarsh Nagar, Delhi - 110033
e-mail : ishabooks@hotmail.com

Laser Typesetting at : Global Printers, New Delhi
Printed at :
Rajdhani Printers, Ph. : 011-23215190

Contents

Preface

Rural development is the process of helping rural people to set the priorities in their own communities through effective and democratic bodies, by providing the local capacity; investment in basic infrastructure and social services; justice, equity and security; dealing with the injustices of the past and ensuring safety and security of the rural population.

In recent years, rural development is getting increased attention in countries around the world. It is one of the most important item in the development agenda of all countries. It contributes greatly to the development of disadvantaged (rural) regions through its various structural funds. A reason for the heightened attention is the deep structural change in rural areas, which includes not only changes in the rural economy, but also serious demographic, social and cultural transitions.

The sustainability of rural development initiatives depends greatly on the capacities of the stake-holders involved, the relationships among them and their relative power. A strategy to foster pluralistic approaches to rural development should focus on building the capacities of those who have been marginalised by development strategies as well as on developing relationships that allow more effective, efficient and equal interactions and greater accountability among all participants. Therefore, the types of changes that are needed to promote substantive and sustainable community-based development are closely associated with more general processes of promoting pluralism and democratisation. Without political space it is exceedingly difficult for local people to organise or have an impact on policy-making processes.

Rural Development: Towards Sustainability is a compilation of three volumes: *Rural Empowerment, Rural Sustainable Development* and *Rural Diversity and Community Development*. Each volume describes the issues and concerns related to its title. It is hoped that this work will address the needs of a wide range of audiences like students, teachers, researchers, policymakers, governmental and non-governamental organisations and all who are directly or indirectly related with rural development.

Editor

1
Agricultural Food Security

Agriculture is an integral part of the general development system, serving the system as a whole, and being served by it. If the effects of other sections of the development systems reduce sustainability, then sustainability of agriculture is also affected. Agriculture is directly linked to very many facets of sustainable development, including poverty eradication, sustainable consumption and production, management of natural resources, energy, freshwater, health, education, trade and market access, as well as technology transfer and capacity building.

A sustainable system should be resilient, and able to withstand shocks and failures of parts of its systems without the whole collapsing, and without small shocks leading to a spiral of unsustainability. Agriculture centres on integrated use of natural resources such as soil, water, climate and biological diversity. The integration of agriculture with other aspects of land management and ecosystem conservation is essential in order to promote both environmental sustainability and agricultural production.

— Natural resources have to be accessible to the poor, which in the farm sector means secure rights to land, water and genetic resources. For this, there is a need to develop public-private partnerships.

— Policies for land and water resource management, biodiversity protection, infrastructure investment, strategy on institutional market reforms, reduction of tariffs and phasing out of possible commodity control are integral to achieving sustainable agriculture.

— Sustainability should be seen in the context of different agro-climatic zones as well of as the country as a whole. Suitable technologies should be developed and indicators for sustainable agriculture should be identified for both.

— It is essential to provide funding for integrated rural development plans, programmes and strategies, at national and regional levels, with particular emphasis on investment in economic and social infrastructure in rural areas, enterprise development, human resource development, and capacity building for local governance.

— An efficient credit policy regime with the required rural banking and credit system will play a major role in the future. The government should encourage investment in vital agriculture infrastructure, credit linkages, and use of new and appropriate techniques towards this end.

— More than 70 per cent of the country's agriculture is under small and marginal farmers with limited resources. A nationwide crop insurance scheme will provide such farmers the needed confidence to invest and gain from technological advances in agriculture.

— The focus on accelerated food grains production on a sustainable basis and free trade in grains, as well as on rural employment opportunities will lead to faster economic growth and give purchasing power to the people, which in turn would help increase household food security.

— Concerted efforts should be made at national, regional and local levels to pool, distil and evaluate traditional practices, knowledge and wisdom and to harness them for sustainable agricultural growth.

— It should be recognized that information is a critical input for agricultural development. It is as important as other key inputs including credit, seeds, nutrients and water. Information can be efficiently converted into economically rewarding opportunities.

— It is critical to recognize that the challenge to world agriculture is both technological, and political.

Equitable Distribution and Access

A positive right to life would imply that the State provides to each and every person, adequate food and other basic necessities, and that it ensures a healthy environment, so that people may live and grow in dignity. The most important challenge in the 1980s and 1990s was physical access to food. In this millennium, the challenge is economic and ecological access to food.

— A transition from chemical and machinery-intensive technologies to ecological farming technologies is required towards providing sustained physical access to food.

— Environmental access involves on the one hand, attention to soil health care, water harvesting and management, conservation of forests and biodiversity, and on the other hand to sanitation, environmental hygiene, primary health care and primary education.

— Emphasis on economic access underlines the need for promoting sustainable livelihoods through multiple income-earning opportunities.

— It is important to increase food availability in areas where it is produced, thus reducing transport costs and excessive dependence on international markets.

— Shift from existing expensive, inefficient and ineffective institutional arrangements, to decentralized management systems of food storage and distribution will improve delivery, reduce handling and transport costs, and reduce corruption, thereby bringing down the issue price substantially.

— Procurement of grain can be decentralized through creation of food grain banks in each village/block of the district, from where people can get subsidized foodgrains (including locally grown coarse cereals) through food coupons.

Food Security

Food security is a physical, environmental, economic and social issue. It involves not just production, but access; not just output but process; not just technology but policy; not just global balance but also national conditions; not just national figures but household realities; not just rural but urban consumption; and not just quantity of food but also quality.

— The concept of food security should be broadened to make it holistic so as to mean "every individual has the physical, economic and environmental access to a balanced diet that includes the necessary macro and micro nutrients and safe drinking water, sanitation, environmental hygiene, primary health care and education so as to lead a healthy and productive life."

— Issues of food security are part of a bigger whole. Sustainable land and water management must be seen as directly linked to food security. Population growth, environmental sustainability, poverty reduction, agricultural production, distribution, marketing, credit and many other factors also need to be recognized as part of this whole. o The major challenge is to produce additional food while conserving depleting natural resources. It is also to provide physical, economic and ecological access to food and nutrition security at the household level.

— Food security must focus on a diversified food basket, not food grains alone. Broad-based food security systems are not dependent on two-three species but on over 100 species that are underutilized. This will also prevent locally adapted grains from becoming extinct.

— Nutrition security must be given integrated attention by emphasizing horticulture, animal husbandry, fishery, millets, pulses and several other resources for which India is traditionally known. There is need for investment in science and technology that will promote diversification. o Food security must not be based on market, but rather on self-reliance and sufficiency. The approach should be one of moving from food security to food sovereignty.

— The elimination of hunger and malnutrition is not just a food problem. It is linked to poverty and population growth. Rising food output is essential but so are the slowing of population growth and maintaining the ecological balance.

— Food banks at grass root levels should be well maintained.

In the 21st century, it is increasingly necessary, and increasingly feasible to take a whole systems approach to organized, positive change in rural places. For extension, that means helping farming people toward sustainably increasing productivity-particularly in the small-mixed farming systems in rain-fed areas, in upland areas, and in other places which have been neglected. It also demands measuring success in terms of the consumption of rural people, as well as of their production.

And that, in turn, will require agricultural extension systems which help farm men and women organize themselves in ways which empower them-to lead agricultural extension and to exert enough power and influence over agricultural research systems so that they generate useful, practical information which fits the needs and interests of those farming people.

— Agricultural extension must focus on increasing production and productivity of food and fiber in an economically and environmentally sustainable way. It must be done in a way which does not destroy rural livelihoods and rural communities.

— Extension activities should promote more comprehensive rural education and extension programmes directed particularly at rural poor, with major emphasis on efforts to reduce illiteracy, particularly among women and girls. o It is important to organize education, extension and information, and skill empowerment on the basis of intensification, diversification and value addition of farming systems.

— Partnerships aimed at strengthening the knowledge base, and improving the dissemination of information, such as farm-to-farm technical assistance programmes, can help strengthen agri-extension. Public-private partnerships could be envisaged in basic sustainable agricultural techniques.

— Sustainable agriculture demonstration plots should be set up in research stations, demonstration centres, seed production centers, farmers' training centres etc., of government, cooperative and non-government agencies.

— The system should support a new agricultural extension system that could meet the needs of information-hungry farmers, especially educated youth and women engaged in farming, and would empower them with new techniques and skills that foster sustainable agriculture.

Awareness and Education Activities

National policies and planning should recognize that public awareness can play an important role in establishing a firm basis for sustainable agricultural resource conservation and use. Public awareness should be considered in the development of all national programme activities.

— National strategies should identify objectives and strategies for public awareness, define target audiences, partners and tools for public outreach.

— Governments should recognize and encourage the work of NGOs in raising public awareness.

— Short-term and long-term courses specializing in sustainable agriculture should be run in agricultural universities. A separate curriculum for this subject should be developed for the regular graduate and postgraduate courses also.

— There is generally public apprehension about the possible consequences of agricultural biotechnology. It is important to organize public information programmes and public discussions that would help share relevant work of agricultural and biological scientists with the public.

Scientific and technological development is not enough in itself. It is critical to make sure that sustainability and poverty reduction remain the guiding principles, and that we use our resources, harness our intellect, and direct our knowledge to benefit the poor, the hungry and the marginalized.

— The impact of agricultural research is decisive. Such research should, wherever possible, be coupled with onfarm activities in order that the context and purpose of the work are fully appreciated. Research should assist in the monitoring, evaluation, and improvement of onfarm efforts.

— Research should be undertaken in a participatory and collaborative manner to foster interaction and cooperation between rural people and research institutions. Other institutions must be involved appropriately whenever necessary.

— A comprehensive area-specific database of natural resources should be developed and made available for agriculture planning, implementation, research and extension. Existing data and information should be assembled, verified, and put in a usable and easily accessible form.

— Well-designed information technology packages should be developed, that could help serve as a market information network; weather, pest and disease monitoring system; and could be a storehouse of various current farming technologies and practices.

— Modern information technology should be used to reach the unreached. Educated youth must be attracted to and retained in farming through spreading science-based precision farming techniques, which are intellectually stimulating and economically rewarding.

— Training and capacity building should be undertaken in areas such as taxonomy, population biology, ethnobotany, and eco-regional and agroecological surveying. Specific research priorities need to be determined separately for each region.

— Additional research is necessary to develop drought tolerant, pest and disease-resistant crops, biological pest management, nitrogen fixation, more effective use of locally available organic materials, inter-cropping systems, and perennial crops, including agroforestry.

— Farming systems need to be designed so as to achieve the triple goals of more food, more income and more livelihoods per hectare of land. For this, it would be fruitful to harness the tools of eco-technologies resulting from a blend of traditional knowledge with frontier technologies. Such tools include biotechnology, information and communication technology, GIS mapping, space technology, renewable energy technologies (solar, wind, biomass, biogas), and management and marketing technologies.

— The revolution in biotechnology has both promises and problems. Biotechnology should be judiciously used so as to support the mission of environmental protection, poverty reduction and food security. But the adoption of every new technology must be accompanied by a precautionary package. In the case of biotechnology, biosafety and biosurviellance must be considered as important factors.

— Food should originate from efficient and environmentally benign production technologies that conserve and enhance the natural resource base of crop and animal husbandry, forestry, inland and marine fisheries.

Value of Agricultural Biodiversity

While a small number of species provides a large proportion of global food needs, hundreds of other species are utilized at a local level, either through cultivation or harvesting. These under-utilized species contribute substantially to household food and livelihood security. They are often managed or harvested by women. Knowledge concerning the uses and management of these species is likewise often localized and specialized. Many under-utilized plants have potential for more widespread use, and their promotion could contribute to food security, agricultural diversification, and income generation, particularly in areas where the cultivation of major crops is economically marginal.

— It is vital to recognize the intrinsic value of biological diversity and of its ecological, social, economic, scientific, educational, cultural, and aesthetic importance. This diversity is being lost in the fields and other ecosystems of virtually all countries.

— High priority needs to be given to safeguarding as much existing unique and valuable diversity as possible in ex-situ collections of plant genetic resources for food and agriculture, and also through in-situ conservation in their natural habitats.

— Goal-oriented, economically efficient and sustainable system of in-situ and ex-situ conservation needs to be developed.

— Cooperation among national programmes and international institutions to sustain in-situ and ex-situ conservation efforts needs to be developed and strengthened. It must be recognized that states have sovereign rights over their own plant and animal genetic resources for food and agriculture.

— A time-bound programme to list, catalogue and classify the country's vast agro-biodiversity with special focus on conserving indigenous breeds and species, must be initiated.

— Agriculture diversity registers should be formed for local and regional varieties. Agriculture policies should be formulated based on these registers.

Relook at Agriculture and Related Policies: It is critical to develop and strengthen appropriate policies and legislative measures to create an enabling environment for sustainable agriculture and rural development. Such an environment would promote access by the poor to land, water resources and other agricultural inputs; land tenure modifications that recognize and protect indigenous and common property resource management systems, and also build local capacities for better management of natural resources.

— Governments should consider, and as appropriate, adopt policies in extension, training, pricing, input distribution, infrastructure development, credit and taxation, which serve as incentives for crop diversification and the creation of markets for biodiverse food crops, including standards for labeling of foods, which allow the highlighting of use of non-standard crop varieties. o Policies should stress on land reforms, input and output pricing, investments in irrigation, infrastructure and insurance, legislation for biodiversity, geographic appellation, varietal protection and farmers' rights. o Well-defined and enforceable land rights, legal security of tenure and equal access to land, water and other natural and biological resources, need to be assured, in particular for indigenous communities, women and disadvantaged people living in poverty.

— It must be recognized that states have sovereign rights over their plant genetic resources for food and agriculture, while also confirming our common and individual responsibilities in respect of these resources.

— Coordination is needed to provide national programmes with information on these issues and to assess the impact of international developments in these fields on the conservation and exchange of plant genetic resources, and to incorporate new research developments, as appropriate, into national systems and practices.

— Effective regulatory mechanisms and safeguards need to be universally installed so that the impacts of biotechnologies are both productive and benign.

— Development of agro-ecology-relevant technologies based on an understanding of local agriculture and resource management practices need to be supported and promoted.

— Chemicals and pesticides banned in developed countries should not be dumped into developing countries in the name of liberalization, globalization and industrialization.

— When patenting a variety or item of research, the area of origin should get due credit and benefit of the patent.

— Before releasing a new variety, including genetically modified varieties in the market, the following parameters should be considered for a variety of agro-climatic zones: Impact on soil productivity; hazardous residual effect; health hazards; adverse effects on other crops; adverse effects on other agricultural practices; threat to the indigenous varieties; impact on other professions; and impact on flora and fauna.

Create Favourable Economic Climate

Agriculture has become a relatively unrewarding profession due to generally unfavourable price regimes and low value addition, causing abandoning of farming and increasing migration from rural areas. The situation is likely to be exacerbated further in the wake of integration of agricultural trade into the global system, unless immediate corrective measures are taken. A favourable economic environment and supportive public management system are the key pillars for the promotion of sustainable agriculture.

— Capital inadequacy, lack of infrastructural support and demand side constraints such as controls on movement, storage and sale of agricultural products, etc. affect the economic viability of agriculture sector. These issues need urgent attention.

— Increasing capital formation and farmer's own investments by removal of distortions in the incentive regime for agriculture, improving the terms of trade with manufacturing sectors and bringing about external and domestic market reforms, backed by rationalization of domestic tax structure, will help to create a favourable economic environment for agriculture.

— Agriculture-dependent countries like India should have a certain degree of autonomy and flexibility in determining the domestic agricultural policies so as to improve productivity, enhance income levels, reduce vulnerability to market fluctuations, ensuring stability of prices, etc.

— Creating a level playing field in the global marketplace will provide the necessary incentives and leeway for farmers, especially the small ones to adopt environmentally friendly farming practices, and help in avoiding, their desperate acts of survival at the expense of sustainable development, due to distortions in international trade.

— In the context of globalization of the food market, farmers in developing countries need to improve access to their own local markets. A 'marketplus' rather than a pure market approach for the agricultural sector would be effective in addressing the wide range of issues associated with production, pricing, food distribution and access.

— At international forums, developing countries like India should have the necessary flexibility to pursue legitimate non-trade concerns with regard to international markets. Such countries should seek reforms in global agricultural policies relating to price, subsidies, trade and technology transfer, and respect for IPRs of local communities.

— International agreements should allow room for the domestic agricultural sector to meet challenges of maintaining the livelihood of the large agriculture-dependent population, and production of sufficient food to meet domestic needs.

— Agricultural food processing industries with international health standards should be promoted locally.

— Biomass based entrepreneurship should be promoted to generate wealth at the rural level.

— Civil society groups should use benchmarks and sustainability indicators to monitor performance of food processors, retailers and food service companies, especially regarding fair terms of trade.

Protection of Rights

National programmes are increasingly confronted with policy, legal and institutional issues related to ownership, intellectual property rights, exchange, transfer and trade in agricultural resources. Participatory processes and involvement of various stakeholders can help find answers to such concerns. Towards this it is crucial to develop a framework for a unified national programme to enhance the diverse efforts within the country to tackle such issues.

— Programmes and policies for food and agriculture activities should involve public and private institutions and companies, non-governmental organizations, communities and individuals from the agriculture, environment and development sectors.

— The role of indigenous and local communities in conserving, collecting, improving and sustainably using plant genetic resources for food and agriculture must be acknowledged. Local, community-level initiatives and participation in proposing programmes need to be encouraged.

— Gender concerns in agriculture need to be mainstreamed. Appropriate structural, functional and institutional measures to empower women and build their capabilities and improve their access to inputs, technologies and other farming resources need to be strengthened.

— The need for equitable sharing of benefits arising from the use of traditional knowledge, innovations and practices relevant to the use and conservation of plant genetic resources for food and agriculture must be recognized.

— Nutrition security must be placed high on the agenda for development plans and programmes at all levels-village, block, district and state. Institutions that will design and monitor locality-specific interventions must be developed.

2

Socially Disadvantaged Groups

According to the 1991 Census, SCs account for 138.2 million, of whom 81 per cent live in rural areas, but spread all over the country, except in the state of Nagaland and the two UTs of Andaman and Nicobar Islands and Lakshadweep. Uttar Pradesh alone accounts for 21.2 per cent of the total SC population in the country. Nearly 84 per cent of total SC population live in ten states viz. Andhra Pradesh (7.7 per cent), Bihar (9.1 per cent), Karnataka (5.3 per cent), Kerala (2.1 per cent), Madhya Pradesh (7.0 per cent), Maharashtra (6.3 per cent), Rajasthan (5.5 per cent), Tamil Nadu (7.8 per cent), Uttar Pradesh (21.2 per cent) and West Bengal (11.6 per cent).

In a few states, they constitute more than 20 per cent of state's total population. These include - Punjab (28.3 per cent), Himachal Pradesh (25.3 per cent), West Bengal (23.6 per cent) and Uttar Pradesh (21.0 per cent). OBCs, as per the Government of India's Notification No. 12011/68/93/BCC© dated 10 September 1993, consist of castes and communities which are common to both the Lists contained in the Report of the Backward Classes Commission (Mandal Commission) and those of the State Governments prepared for the purpose. So far, Central Lists of OBCs in respect of 21 States and 5 UTs have been notified.

The Minorities, as per the 1991 Census, constitute 145.31 million or 17.2 per cent of the total population of the country. While Muslims represent 12 per cent of the total population, Christians account for 2.3 per cent, Sikhs 2 per cent and Buddhists 0.8 per cent. The Zoroastrians number around 1 lakh. The Muslims constitute 94.3 per cent of total population in Lakshadweep, 64 per cent in Jammu & Kashmir, 28.4 per cent in Assam, 23.6 per cent in West Bengal and 23.3 per cent in Kerala, far above the national level average. A sizeable Muslim population is also found in Uttar Pradesh (25 million), West Bengal (18 million) and Bihar (13 million). The 20 million Christian population is predominantly found in Mizoram (85.5 per cent of the state's population)), Meghalaya (64.8 per cent) and Nagaland (87.6 per cent).

There is also a substantial Christian population in Kerala, Tamil Nadu, Goa and the Union Territory of Andaman & Nicobar Islands. The Sikhs, numbering about 16 million, constitute 63 per cent of the population in Punjab and 20 per cent of the population in the Union Territory of Chandigarh. Their population ranges between 1 and 6 per cent of the population in Himachal Pradesh, Rajasthan and Haryana, while it is below 1 per cent elsewhere in the country. The total population of Buddhists in the country is 6.76 million. There are two categories of Buddhists in the country. The traditional Buddhists are concentrated in the hilly areas of Ladakh, Madhya Pradesh, West Bengal, Sikkim and Arunachal Pradesh, while the newly converted Buddhists are mainly found in Maharashtra (6.3 per cent of the state's population), Uttar Pradesh (0.2 per cent), Madhya Pradesh (0.3 per cent) and West Bengal (0.3 per cent).

The largest Buddhist concentration is in Sikkim, which has 27 per cent of the total Buddhist population in the country, followed by Arunachal Pradesh with 13 per cent. The presence of Zoroastrians is very negligible in most of the states, except for Maharashtra (about 60,000), Gujarat (about 13,000), West Bengal, Andhra Pradesh and Daman & Diu, where their number is about 3,000 in each.

Constitutional Safeguards

Recognising the relative backwardness of these weaker sections of the society, the Constitution of India guarantees equality before the law (Article 14) and enjoins the State to make special provisions for the advancement of any socially and educationally backward classes or for SCs (Article 15(4)). It also empowers the State to make provisions for reservation in appointments or posts in favour of any backward class of citizens (Article (16(4)). The Constitution of India also states categorically that untouchability is abolished and its practice in any form is forbidden (Article 17).

Further, it enjoins the State to promote, with special care, the educational and economic interests of the weaker sections of the people and, in particular, of SCs and promises to protect them from social injustice and all forms of exploitation (Article 46). Reservation of seats for SCs in the democratic institutions (Article 330) and in services (Article 335) is another measure of positive discrimination in favour of these Groups. It empowers the State to appoint a Commission to investigate into the conditions of socially and educationally backward classes (Article 340) and to specify the Castes to be deemed as SCs (Article 341).

In the case of Minorities, the Constitution adopts certain safeguards to recognise their rights in conserving their culture and establish and administer educational institutions of their choice under the Articles 29 and 30. While the Article 350(A) advocates instructions in the mother tongue at the primary stage of education to children belonging to Linguistic Minorities, Article 350(B) provides for a Special Officer to safeguard the interests of the Linguistic Minorities. Besides these specific Articles, there are also a number of Constitutional provisions enabling protection and promotion of the interests of these Socially Disadvantaged Groups.

Policies and Programmes

The developmental planning launched in 1951 through the First Plan (1951-56) envisaged that the programmes under various sectors of development would benefit all sections of the population including SCs, OBCs and Minorities. But, unfortunately, it never happened so. Therefore, special programmes under the Backward Classes Sector were formulated, keeping in view the special requirements of SCs. The Second Plan (1956-61) promised to ensure that the benefits of economic development accrue more and more to the relatively less privileged classes of society in order to reduce inequalities. The Third Plan (1961-66) advocated greater 'equality of opportunity' and a reduction in disparities in income and wealth and the even distribution of economic power.

The Fourth and Fifth Plans (1969-78) envisaged the 'basic goal as rapid increase in the standard of living of the people through measures which also prómote equality and social justice'. One of the important features of the subsequent Annual Plan (1979-80) was the launching of the special mechanism of Special Component Plan (SCP) for SCs to ensure that these groups receive their due share of funds/benefits from the other developmental sectors. The Sixth Plan (1980-85) marked a shift in the approach to the development of SCs. Special emphasis was laid on the implementation of the newly launched SCP for SCs facilitating easy convergence and pooling of resources from all the other developmental sectors in proportion to the population of SCs and monitoring of various developmental programmes for the benefit of SCs.

In the Seventh Plan (1985-90), SCP for SCs was strengthened, while the other schemes for the welfare and development of SCs continued. There was a substantial increase in the flow of funds for the development of SCs under SCP from State Plans, Central Plans, Special Central Assistance (SCA) and Institutional Finance resulting in the expansion of infrastructural facilities and enlargement of their coverage. Priority in the Seventh Plan was given to the educational development of SCs. Another important achievement of this Plan was the setting up of a National Scheduled Castes and Scheduled Tribes Finance and Development Corporation (NSFDC) in 1989 to extend loans-cum-subsidies and thus encourage these Groups to become gainfully engaged in various income-generation activities.

The major objective of the Eighth Plan (1992-97) was to intensify the efforts and to bridge the gap between the development of SCs, OBCs and Minorities and other sections of the society, so that by the turn of the century these disadvantaged sections of the population could be brought on par with the rest of the society. It was envisaged that all forms of oppression of SCs, suppression of their rights, untouchability, non-payment of minimum wages etc., would be eliminated, so as to enable them to avail of the benefits of all developmental efforts. Although the efforts have paid dividends with regard to improvement of socio-economic status of these groups, the benefits were, however, not evenly distributed among all communities. As such, a lot remains to be done to achieve the goal of bringing these groups on par with the rest of the society.

For the economic development of SCs, OBCs and Minorities, the following three Nationallevel Apex bodies were set up to act as catalytic agents in developing schemes for employment generation and financing pilot projects viz. i) The National Backward Classes Finance and Development Corporation; ii) The National Minorities Development and Finance Corporation; and iii) National Safai Karamchari Finance and Development Corporation.

The Ninth Plan was committed to empower the Socially Disadvantaged Groups as agents of socio-economic change and development through - creating an enabling environment conducive for SCs, OBCs and Minorities to exercise their rights freely, enjoy their privileges and be able to lead a life with confidence and dignity on par with the rest of the society; ensuring removal of disparities; eliminating exploitation and suppression and providing protection to the disadvantaged groups; ensuring developmental benefits to 'reach the un-reached' through equitable distribution and social justice; ensuring participation of these Groups in the process of planning not merely as beneficiaries but also as participants in planning programmes and their implementation; accelerating the on-going process of improving socio-economic status through the effective implementation of various policies and programmes to bring them on par with the rest of the society; and ensuring a certain percentage of funds/benefits from all the relevant programmes to flow to women belonging to these groups who are the most affected.

As most of the Ministries/Departments implement programmes common for both SCs and Scheduled Tribes (STs), including earmarking of a percentage of funds/benefits under SCP for SCs and Tribal Sub-Plan (TSP) for STs. The approach adopted towards empowering these Groups in the Ninth Plan was holistic in nature, to accomplish their all round development through (i) Social Empowerment; (ii) Economic Empowerment; and (iii)

Social Justice with an inter-sectoral focus and inputs from both governmental and non-governmental agencies. The same is sought to be achieved through the efforts put in by various welfare-related Ministries/ Departments and the nodal Ministry of Social Justice & Empowerment which is responsible for the development of SCs, OBCs and Minorities. They include the following:

Education and Literacy

Education being the most powerful instrument for empowering the Socially Disadvantaged Groups, the Ninth Plan committed to achieve the same through universalisation of primary education by 2005 with a special focus on low-literacy pockets and on the educationally backward communities like SCs, OBCs and Minorities. In pursuance of the commitments made by the National Policy on Education, 1986 and in recognition of education as a Fundamental Right (yet to be announced), the Department of Education continued to take various steps to reduce drop-out rates and increase school enrolment and retention rates amongst the children belonging to SCs, OBCs and Minorities.

The following special provisions for SCs have been incorporated in the existing schemes of the Departments of Elementary Education & Literacy and Secondary Education & Higher Education - relaxed norms for opening of primary schools; a primary school within one km walking distance from habitations of 200 population instead of habitations of 300 population; and abolition of tuition fee in Government schools in all states, at least up to the primary level. Most of the states have already abolished tuition fee for SC students up to the Senior Secondary level, along with incentives like provision of free textbooks, uniforms, stationery, school bags etc. to these students.

The other major programmes of the Department of Elementary Education & Literacy having relevance to SCs and OBCs include - the District Primary Education Programme (DPEP), Lok Jumbish, Shiksha Karmi, Non-Formal Education (NFE) and National Programme for Nutritional Support to Primary Education (popularly known as Mid-Day Meals). One of the strategies of the programme of Sarva Shiksha Abhiyan (SSA) is the educational development of children belonging to SCs, OBCs and educationally-backward Minorities.

SSA is a historic stride towards achieving the long cherished goal of Universalisation of Elementary Education (UEE) through a time-bound integrated approach, in partnership with the states. SSA aims to universalise elementary education to cover all children in the 6-14 age-group by 2010 through the community-owned and mission-mode approach. It also envisages bridging of gender and social gaps through a special focus on the children of SCs, STs and other disadvantaged groups. The DPEP aims mainly at providing access to primary education for all children, reducing primary drop-out rates to less than 10 per cent and increasing learning achievement of primary school students by at least 25 per cent. It is also meant to reduce the gap among gender and social groups to less than 5 per cent.

The NFE programme lays emphasis on girls, working children and those belonging to SCs. At present, there are 2,92,000 NFE centres covering about 7.3 million children in 25 States/UTs. The major thrust of the National Literacy Mission, which aims to attain full literacy, i.e. a sustainable threshold level of 75 per cent by 2005, is on the promotion of literacy among women, SCs, STs and OBCs. This is reflected in the fact that a high 61 per cent of learners are females, while 23 per cent belong to SCs and 13 per cent to STs.

Janshala, yet another community-based primary education programme, aims to make primary education more accessible and effective, especially for girls and children of deprived communities, marginalised groups, SCs, STs, Minorities, working children and children with special needs. Janshala is a block-based programme with emphasis on community participation and decentralisation. This is the first ever programme in the world where five United Nations agencies have collaborated and pooled resources to support an initiative in education. The programme now covers 105 blocks in 9 states - Andhra Pradesh, Chhattisgarh, Jharkhand, Karnataka, Madhya Pradesh, Maharashtra, Orissa, Rajasthan and Uttar Pradesh - with a total project outlay of Rs. 98.29 crore. Janshala programme is to run for five years from 1998 to 2002.

To enable SC and ST students to pursue higher technical studies, the following special provisions have been extended by the Department of Secondary & Higher Education : reservation of seats for SCs/STs in the Central Government institutions of higher education, including Indian Institutes of Technology (IITs), Indian Institutes of Management (IIMs), Regional Engineering Colleges (RECs), Central Universities, Kendriya Vidyalayas and Navodaya Vidyalayas, etc.; relaxation in the minimum qualifying cut-off percentages for admission to universities, colleges and technical institutions; remedial and special coaching for SC/ ST students to improve academic skills and linguistic proficiency and raise their level of comprehension.

The IITs have a scheme to provide one year's preparatory course for SC/ST students who fail marginally in the entrance examination. Out of 43,000 scholarships at the secondary stage for talented children from rural areas, 13,000 are reserved exclusively for SC/ ST students. Besides, 70 scholarships are reserved exclusively for SC/ ST students under the National Talent Search Scheme. SC/ST candidates are provided relaxation up to 10 per cent of cut-off marks for the Junior Research Fellowship (JRF) test and all SC/ST candidates qualifying for the JRF are awarded fellowships. Around 50 Junior Fellowships are awarded every year in sciences to SC/ST candidates who appear in the National Eligibility Test (NET) and qualify the eligibility test for lecturership.

Also, special attention is being paid to 146 districts identified as low female literacy districts. The scheme of Area-Intensive Programme for Educationally Backward Minorities provides basic infrastructure and facilities in the areas with a concentration of educationally backward minorities and which do not have adequate provision for elementary and secondary education. Under this scheme, 100 per cent financial assistance is given to State Governments and voluntary organisations for the establishment of new primary/upper primary schools and multi-stream residential higher secondary schools for girls belonging to those groups. The scheme covers 325 Blocks in 13 states and 3 UTs and 4 districts in Assam.

To enhance skills and linguistic proficiency in various subjects, special coaching is provided to SC students. The scheme is in operation in 26 universities and 449 colleges. Coaching for students belonging to educationally backward minority communities to compete in various competitive examinations is being provided through 77 coaching centres, including 10 coaching centres for women functioning in 22 universities and 55 colleges.

To facilitate educational development amongst the Minorities, the Scheme for Modernisation of Madarsa Education continues to encourage traditional institutions like Madarsas and Maktabs to introduce Science, Mathematics, Social Studies, Hindi and English in their curriculum. Hundred per cent financial assistance is provided for the appointment of qualified teachers.

Health and Family Welfare

The National Health Policy (1983) accorded high priority for extending health services to those residing in the backward rural areas, with a concentration of SCs. It laid special emphasis on endemic diseases. National Malaria Eradication Programme including Filaria Control, Japanese Encephalitis Control and Kala-azar Control were implemented by States/UTs with 50 per cent central assistance for spraying insecticides, supply of Anti-Malaria drugs etc. in the areas of SC concentration under SCP. The National Leprosy Eradication Programme is 100 per cent centrally assisted programme for the detection and treatment of leprosy cases. This programme has been in action in all districts of the country and covers the entire SC population.

The National Tuberculosis Control Programme (NTCP) implemented with central assistance, supplies anti-TB drugs, equipment etc. to areas with high concentration of SCs/STs under SCP/TSP. Further, the norms of NTCP were relaxed and the following steps were taken for facilitating effective service delivery in rural/tribal areas for -

i) providing Senior Treatment Supervisors and Senior Tuberculosis Laboratories Supervisors for 2-3 lakh population against the established norms of 5 lakh;

ii) opening of microscopic centres for 50,000 population against the established norms of 1 lakh;

iii) opening of more Direct Observation Therapy (DOT) Centres; and

iv) provision to reimburse the travel claims of patients and attendants for taking treatment at DOT Centres.

Under the National Programme on Control of Blindness, 100 per cent central assistance is being extended for strengthening of ophthalmic infrastructure, training of personnel, etc. in areas with SC concentration for treatment of eye ailments and control of blindness under SCP. The National AIDS Control Programme is implemented in areas with sizeable SC population, though no separate provision is made for SCP.

Labour and Employment

In the field of Labour and Employment, the Ministry of Labour is implementing special training and rehabilitation programmes for SCs to equip them with necessary training in upgradation of skills and, thus, improve their employment opportunities. The scheme of 'Coaching-cum-Guidance Centre for SCs/STs' was implemented through 22 centres in various States/UTs to provide occupational information as well as individual guidance and to conduct confidence-building programmes for the benefit of the SC/ST job seekers.

To facilitate the recruitment of SC/ST candidates against reserved vacancies in various Central Government Ministries/Departments, the Directorate-General of Employment and Training (DGET) has launched another scheme, viz. 'Special Coaching Scheme' in 1973 for SC/ST job-seekers registered with the employment exchanges to enable them to appear in Competitive Examinations/Selection Tests conducted for recruitment in Group C and equivalent posts.

The scheme was launched on a pilot basis at Delhi and Ghaziabad and so far 17 phases of this programme have been completed and the 18th phase is in progress since January, 2000. Encouraged with the success of the above scheme, the scheme has been extended to 12 more places through the Coaching-cum-Guidance Centres located at Bangalore, Kolkata, Hyderabad, Ranchi, Surat, Kanpur, Guwahati, Imphal, Hissar, Jabalpur, Chennai and Thiruvananthapuram. Further, a number of welfare schemes for providing medical, housing, educational, recreational and family welfare benefits are being implemented under the Labour Welfare Funds with special dispensation for SC and ST workers engaged in mining.

Also, 15 per cent of the houses built by mining managements are reserved for SCs/STs. Under the Integrated Housing Scheme for Beedi Workers, the exclusive ownership of land is not insisted upon in respect of SCs/STs. Under the Scheme 'Award of Scholarships to the Wards of Miners and Beedi Workers', reservation for SC/ST students is provided on the basis of percentage of SC/ST population in the district, subject to a floor of 15 per cent for SCs and 7.5 per cent for STs. The minimum marks for eligibility under the scholarship scheme for SCs are 35 per cent, against 45 per cent in case of other students.

Thus, education and housing have been identified as the major thrust areas and the tempo of the welfare schemes relating to them have been substantially stepped up with the consequential benefits flowing in greater measure to the SCs/ STs. The rehabilitation of bonded labour has a special significance for SCs and STs, as these communities constitute 61.5 per cent and 25.1 per cent respectively of bonded labour in the country as per the Report of the National Commission on Rural Labour, 1991. According to reports received from State Governments of Andhra Pradesh, Arunachal Pradesh, Bihar (including Jharkhand), Gujarat, Haryana, Karnataka, Kerala, Madhya Pradesh (including Chhattisgarh), Maharashtra, Orissa, Rajasthan, Tamil Nadu and Uttar Pradesh (including Uttaranchal) as many as 2.8 lakh bonded labourers have been identified and out of these 2.6 lakh have been rehabilitated up to March 2001. A separate SC Development Planning Cell has been functioning under the Ministry, since 1981 to co-ordinate the policy, planning and monitoring.

Women and Child Development

Programmes for women and children implemented by the Department of Women and Child Development are primarily directed towards the most disadvantaged groups of population like SCs, STs and other economically backward classes living in backward rural areas, tribal areas and urban slums. The basic consideration of all the schemes is to ensure that the benefits flow to women and children belonging to the disadvantaged sections of the population. The Department has been implementing one of the largest area-based programme of Integrated Child Development Services (ICDS). It aims to provide a package of 6 basic services of health, immunisation, supplementary feeding, referral services, nonformal pre-school education and health and nutrition education - for children below 6 years and for expectant and nursing mothers living in the most backward and rural areas and urban slums with high concentration of severely disadvantaged groups.

By the end of the Ninth Plan, ICDS is expected to be universalised by covering all the 5,652 Blocks/ Wards to benefit 54.3 million children and 10.9 million mothers. Most of the evaluation studies have indicated that out of the total beneficiaries under the schemes, about 78 per cent belong to SCs. Also, under the scheme of Hostels for Working Women implemented by the Department, there are stipulations to reserve 15 per cent of seats for SCs.

Rural Development

The Ministry of Rural Development plays a vital role in raising the status of the poor above the poverty line and improving the quality of life in rural areas through the implementation of various poverty alleviation programmes and providing avenues for self/wage employment to the most disadvantaged Groups, viz. SCs, STs and others. Under the Jawahar Gram Samriddhi Yojana (JGSY), which provides wage employment, 22.5 per cent of Plan allocation is earmarked for SC/ST families living 'Below the Poverty Line' (BPL).

During the Ninth Plan, 395.6 million man-days were provided for SCs, accounting for 28.5 per cent of total employment under this scheme. Under the Employment Assurance Scheme (EAS) which is open to all rural poor who are in need of wage-employment, preference is given to SCs/STs and parents of child labour withdrawn from hazardous occupations who are below the poverty line. Around 500 million mandays were provided to SCs during the Ninth Plan under EAS, accounting for 33.7 per cent of total employment provided under the scheme. JGSY and EAS have been brought under the purview of the mega scheme of Sampoorna Gramin Rozgar Yojana (SGRY) since September 2001.

For taking up self-employment and incomegeneration activities, Swarnajayanti Gram Swarozgar Yojana (SGSY) stipulates that at least 50 per cent of the swarozgaris will be from SCs/ STs. Under SGSY, 1.8 million SC swarozgaris accounting for 32.5 per cent of the total number of swarozgaris, benefited during the Ninth Plan. In addition to these poverty alleviation programmes, this Ministry also provides basic amenities like housing, drinking water, etc. Indira Awas Yojana (IAY) has the objective of providing dwelling units to BPL rural households belonging primarily to SCs, along with STs. About 1.8 million dwelling units were constructed for SCs accounting for 47.4 per cent of total houses under the scheme during the Ninth Plan.

Around 60 per cent of the total allocation was earmarked for SCs/STs. Under the Credit-cum-Subsidy scheme of rural housing, a minimum of 60 per cent of the funds allocated as subsidy to each state has been earmarked for the construction of houses for SCs/STs. Under the Accelerated Rural Water Supply Programme (ARWSP), states are required to utilise a minimum of 25 per cent of funds for provision of drinking water supply to SCs. Around 23.1 million SCs have been benefited, accounting for 18.1 per cent of total beneficiaries under ARSWP. Under the Central Rural Sanitation Programme (CRSP), sanitary latrines are provided to rural population with preference to SC/ST families and people below the poverty line.

A minimum of 20 per cent of the total funds is earmarked for providing subsidy to individual BPL households belonging to SCs and STs. Where such households are more than 20 per cent of the total population, earmarking is enhanced at least to match the percentage of SC population. During the Ninth Plan, one million (21.2 per cent) sanitary latrines were provided to SCs. The National Social Assistance Programme (NSAP), comprising the National Old Age Pensions Scheme (NOAPS), the National Family Benefit Scheme (NFBS) and the National Maternity Benefit Scheme (NMBS) introduces a national policy for social security assistance to the poor SC/ST families and represents a significant step forward.

During the Ninth Plan, 7.8 million SCs were covered under NOAPS, accounting for 24.4 per cent of total 32.2 million beneficiaries. Of the total one million beneficiaries of the NFBS, 2 lakh (20.2 per cent) comprised of SC families. NMBS (now transferred to Department of Family Welfare w.e.f. 2001-02) benefited 1.2 million SC women, who accounted for 21.8 per cent of the total 5.6 million beneficiaries.

Urban Development

The special scheme of Urban Self-Employment Programme under Swarna Jayanti Shahari Rozgar Yojana (SJSRY) extends assistance to the urban poor living below the poverty line with special attention to women and persons belonging to SCs and STs to set up gainful selfemployment ventures. The benefits for SCs are granted keeping in view the extent of the proportion of their strength in the local population. The National Agenda for Governance identified 'Housing for All' as a major programme with special emphasis on the needs of the vulnerable groups wherein it was proposed to facilitate construction of 20 lakh additional units every year, with emphasis on the Economically Weaker Sections and Low Income Groups as also the needs of SCs/STs.

A special Cell in the Ministry of Urban Development and Poverty Alleviation monitors the implementation of the various Government Orders regarding reservation in services for SCs/STs through periodical returns. In addition, the Cell also monitors the filling up of the backlog of vacancies reserved for SCs, STs and OBCs under the Special Recruitment Drive in respect of the Attached/ Subordinate Offices and the Public Sector Undertakings of this Ministry.

Social Justice and Empowerment

Supplementing and complementing the efforts of the sectoral Ministries/Departments, the nodal Ministry of Social Justice & Empowerment continued to work through promoting educational and economic development, besides extending necessary protective measures.

Educational Development

Greater emphasis was laid in the Ninth Plan on the educational development of SCs. The nation-wide popular scheme of 'Post-Matric Scholarships (PMS) for SC Students', the largest educational scholarship scheme of its kind in the country, continued to promote higher education amongst SCs. The scheme extends scholarships to all eligible SC students who pursue postmatriculation courses in recognised institutions. The revision of the scheme in 1997-98 expanded its scope for enhancing the income ceiling of parents of the beneficiaries and for extending some additional benefits to persons with disabilities amongst SCs.

Scholarships are given to all the eligible SC students based on a Means Test which includes provision of maintenance allowance, reimbursement of compulsory non-refundable fees, thesis typing/printing charges, study tour charges, book allowance for students pursuing correspondence courses etc. An expenditure of Rs. 457.29 crore was incurred benefiting around 21 lakh SC students studying at the Post-Matric and above levels, including the professional/technical courses. An evaluation study on the scheme conducted by the Ministry reveals that SC students in some states are facing hardships due to non-payment of scholarships in time, as the State Governments could not meet the expenditure on committed liability under the scheme.

The Scheme of 'Pre-Matric Scholarship for the Children of those engaged in Unclean Occupations' aims to motivate the children of scavengers, sweepers, flayers and tanners to pursue education and also to reduce school dropout rates amongst them. Special provisions for students with disabilities were also introduced keeping in line with the provisions of the Persons with Disabilities Act, 1995. Against the total Ninth Plan outlay of Rs. 30 crore, for the scheme, the expenditure was Rs. 36.25 crore. The scheme covered 19.2 lakh beneficiaries, 2.3 lakh more than the target of 16.9 lakh beneficiaries. An evaluation report on the performance of the scheme has revealed that the programme is instrumental in encouraging many people who are living below the poverty line to send their children to the schools.

The scheme of 'Hostels for SC Boys and Girls' launched in 1961-62, being one of the major support services to improve enrolment, aims at reducing the present high drop-out rates and increasing retention amongst SC/ST students by providing them hostel facilities in the middle, secondary and higher secondary schools, colleges and universities. The central assistance to the scheme has been declining, as the State Governments are not able to provide the required matching share under this scheme. Evaluation of the scheme carried out by the Ministry reveals that the performance of some states in providing matching grants, maintenance of services and management of hostels is not encouraging.

Also, the basic amenities therein are substandard due to poor maintenance of buildings. As against the total Ninth Plan outlay of Rs. 97.05 crore for the scheme, the expenditure was Rs. 118.10 crore for the construction of 354 girls' hostels and 388 boys' hostels benefiting 25,196 SC girls and 17,244 SC boys. The scheme of 'Special Educational Development Programmes for SC Girls belonging to Low Literacy Districts', introduced in 1996-97, aims to establish special residential schools for SC Girls who are first generation learners from low literacy pockets where the traditions and environment are not conducive to learning.

The scheme covers 48 districts spread over Bihar, Madhya Pradesh, Rajasthan and Uttar Pradesh where the literacy amongst SC girls was less than 2 per cent, as per

1981 Census. Central assistance is given to Zilla Parishads to run the schools by themselves or through credible Non-Government Organisations (NGOs). Of the Ninth Plan allocation of Rs. 7.70 crore, the expenditure was only Rs. 1.61 crore, and against a target of 140 schools, only 104 schools could be funded. The 'Book Banks Scheme for SC/ST Students' continued to supply text-books to SC students for pursuing Medical, Engineering, Veterinary, Agricultural, Polytechnic, Chartered Accountancy, Business Administration, Bio-Sciences and Law Courses. Provision has also been made for Braille Books to visually disabled SC students.

Against the total Ninth Plan outlay of Rs. 12 crore for the scheme, the expenditure was Rs. 10.61 crore for benefiting about 1.15 lakh SC/ST students. The scheme of 'Up-gradation of Merit of SC/ST Students' aims to provide remedial and special coaching to SC students studying in classes IX to XII. While the remedial coaching aims at helping SC students weak in some school subjects, special coaching helps them to prepare for appearing in competitive examinations and for admission tests for professional courses like medicine, engineering etc. The Ninth Plan allocation of Rs. 5.26 crore was later raised to Rs. 42.50 crore which was earmarked for 2001-02 with a view to assisting 25,000 SC/ST students from Classes VI to Degree/Diploma-level courses.

But, unfortunately, the expenditure was Rs. 4.72 crore only for benefiting 3,755 SC students. Despite the Centre's willingness to bear the entire cost, most of the States/UTs failed to respond favourably for implementing the scheme. Therefore, the scheme had very limited impact in achieving its objective. Coaching and Allied Scheme for SC/ST students which aims to improve the knowledge and aptitude of SC/ST students by providing special coaching to them through Pre-Examination Training Centres (PETCs), was recast during the Ninth Plan by bringing revision in the unit-cost. Universities and private institutions receive 100 per cent Central assistance on a contractual basis, while Stateowned PETCs receive the Central assistance to the extent of 50 per cent of the contractual amount.

The scheme, which was common for both SC and ST students till the year 2000-01, is now exclusively meant for SC students, after a separate Ministry of Tribal Affairs was set up in 1999. Of the Ninth Plan outlay of Rs. 16.71 crore for the scheme, the expenditure was Rs. 11.09 crore for coaching and training for 48,500 SC/ST students. Educational development of OBCs, which made a beginning during the 1990s, received better attention during the Ninth Plan with many new initiatives coming up in the field of education. Towards ensuring educational development amongst OBCs, schemes for providing scholarships for pursuing both Pre-Matric and Post-Matric as well as other higher education, supported with hostel facilities, were introduced.

Besides, children belonging to the OBCs were also allowed to enjoy the existing hostel facilities meant for SC boys and girls. For OBC students to participate effectively in the competitive examinations, Pre-Examination Coaching Centres were also set up in the Ninth Plan. The scheme of Post-Matric Scholarships for OBC Students is intended to promote higher education amongst OBCs by extending financial support to poor OBC students studying at the level of matriculation and above, including Ph.D degrees etc. Of the Ninth Plan allocation of Rs. 49.90 crore, an expenditure of Rs. 40.57 crore was incurred benefiting 5.8 lakh OBC students. So far, only 15 states viz. Andhra Pradesh, Assam, Bihar, Goa, Himachal Pradesh, Jammu and Kashmir, Jharkhand, Karnataka, Madhya Pradesh, Maharashtra, Manipur, Sikkim, Tripura, Uttaranchal and Uttar Pradesh could avail the benefit of this scheme.

The scheme of Pre-Matric Scholarships for OBC Students aims to motivate children of OBCs studying at pre-matric stage in recognised schools. Of the Ninth Plan outlay of Rs. 49.90 crore for the scheme, the expenditure was Rs. 29.15 crore, benefiting 12.6 lakh OBC students. The states of Andhra Pradesh, Assam, Bihar, Jammu & Kashmir, Jharkhand, Karnataka, Madhya Pradesh, Manipur, Sikkim, Tripura and Uttar Pradesh could utilise the funds under this scheme. The scheme of Hostels for OBC Boys and Girls, being one of the major support services aims to reduce the high drop-out rate at middle/ higher university level education amongst OBCs with the objective of providing accommodation with congenial atmosphere. Of the Ninth Plan outlay of Rs. 49.90 crore for the scheme, expenditure incurred was only Rs. 20.76 crore, benefiting 11,470 students.

The State Governments of Andhra Pradesh, Bihar, Jharkhand, Karnataka, Madhya Pradesh, Manipur, Rajasthan, Sikkim, Tripura, Tamil Nadu and Uttar Pradesh could utilise funds under this scheme. The scheme for Pre-Examination Coaching for OBCs was introduced with a major objective of providing special coaching/training for OBC candidates to help compete in competitive examinations for recruitment to various services. The candidates, whose parents' total annual income from all sources is below Rs. 1 lakh are eligible for admission to this special coaching scheme. Of the Ninth Plan allocation of Rs. 10 crore, only Rs. 1.03 crore has been spent benefiting 2,480 students.

The scheme of Assistance to Voluntary Organisations for the Welfare of OBCs was launched with a major objective of involving the voluntary sector for improving the educational and economic conditions of OBCs. Of the Ninth Plan allocation of Rs. 10 crore, for the scheme, the expenditure was Rs. 1.03 crore to assist 20,880 beneficiaries. For Minorities, education has become a key input in their development, as a large section amongst them continues to be educationally backward. Improvement in literacy levels, upgradation of the quality of education and its relevance to the emerging employment opportunities are crucial to their development.

Initiatives taken in this direction are enumerated: The Maulana Azad Education Foundation was set up as an autonomous organisation in 1992-93 with the objective of promoting education amongst educationally backward sections in general and Minorities in particular. The Foundation provides for remedial coaching, construction/ expansion of schools/residential schools/ colleges/ polytechnics/hostels mainly for girls and purchase of machinery/equipment for laboratories and for setting up/strengthening vocational/technical training centres for women. As against the total Ninth Plan outlay of Rs. 70 crore, Rs. 52.75 crore was spent to assist about 417 NGOs.

The scheme of Pre-Examination Coaching for Weaker Sections, based on economic criteria, is extended to enable them to compete on equal terms with other candidates in competitive examinations for various jobs and it is being implemented through the Institutions of repute. Against a provision of Rs. 12 crore for the Ninth Plan, Rs. 11.29 crore was spent for funding 417 Institutions to train 30,310 students.

Economic Development

The National Scheduled Castes and Scheduled Tribes Finance and Development Corporation (NSFDC) continued to function as a catalytic agent for financing, facilitating and mobilising funds from various sources for promoting economic development activities amongst SCs living below double the poverty line. Financial assistance, at a concessional rate of interest, is extended to the target groups for taking up viable economic activities through the 34 State Channelising Agencies, which include Scheduled Caste Development Corporations (SCDCs) and other recognised financial institutions. Skill and entrepreneurial training is also imparted to unemployed SC youths through reputed training institutions.

A micro-credit scheme has also been taken up since 2000-01 for funding Self-Help Groups (SHGs) by which small loans are provided to the target groups through NGOs. The Authorised Share Capital of the Corporation was Rs. 300 crore and it was raised to Rs. 1,000 crore in 1999-2000. Its paid-up share capital is now Rs. 421 crore. The Corporation has so far sanctioned 2,759 projects, which on completion, would enable 3.4 lakh SC beneficiaries to take up various employment-cumincome-generating activities. During the last year of the Ninth Plan (2001-02), NSFDC was bifurcated into 2 separate Corporations - one for SCs and the other for STs viz. National Scheduled Castes Finance and Development Corporation for SCs and National Scheduled Tribes Finance and Development Corporation for STs.

SCDCs are playing a key role at state level as guarantors, promoters and catalysts for generating credit from financial institutions and providing missing inputs by way of margin money loans and subsidy to SCs living below the poverty line. At present, these Corporations are functioning in 25 States/UTs. This Scheme was revised in 1998-99 with a view to ensuring effective utilisation of central assistance extended to the states. Of the Ninth Plan allocation of Rs. 180 crore, an expenditure of Rs. 173.63 crore was incurred for extending financial assistance to 14.88 lakh SCs. The National Safai Karamcharis Finance and Development Corporation (NSKFDC) was set up in January 1997 as a non-profit making company exclusively for promoting economic development/ self-employment amongst the scavenging communities. NSKFDC acts as an apex institution for channelising funds through the State Channelising Agencies.

Financial assistance on concessional rates is provided to persons engaged in scavenging occupations for the establishment of alternative viable income-generation activities. Under the Micro-Credit Scheme, introduced in 2000-01, Safai Karamcharis were organised into SHGs with the help of State Channelising Agencies/ NGOs to receive loans to a maximum of Rs. 10,000 per beneficiary for undertaking income-generation activities. Financial assistance is also extended to Co-operatives formed by a group of 25 scavengers for setting up of Sanitary Marts production-cumservice centres and for conversion of dry latrines into wet ones. The Ninth Plan allocation of Rs. 81.75 crore has been released to the NSKFDC and the scheme has benefited 33,725 persons. The National Backward Classes Finance and Development Corporation (NBCFDC) was set up in 1992 with a major objective of promoting selfemployment ventures and income-generation activities among the poorest of OBCs living below double the poverty line.

The Corporation provides loans at concessional rates of interest and also arranges training for upgradation of technological and entrepreneurial skills amongst the individuals or groups belonging to OBCs through the State Channelising Agencies. The initial Authorized Share Capital of Rs. 200 crore has been raised to Rs. 700 crore. The Corporation has disbursed term loans to the tune of Rs. 614.08 crore to assist 3.75 lakh beneficiaries during the Ninth Plan. A micro-credit scheme has also been introduced for extending credit facilities to the target groups for small business especially for women beneficiaries through State Channelising Agencies as well as NGOs. It has also launched a special scheme, viz.

'Swarnima' for providing a loan upto Rs. 1 lakh for self-employment activities. Of the Ninth Plan allocation of Rs. 400 crore for the NBCFDC, Rs. 191.50 crore was spent for the activities.

The National Minorities Development and Finance Corporation (NMDFC) was set up in 1994-95 to promote income generating activities among the poorest of the poor in the minority groups. The Corporation provides loans at concessional rates of interest and organises training programmes, especially for the craftsmen engaged in traditional occupations and trades. The Corporation operates all the programmes through networking with the State Channelising Agencies. The authorised share capital of the Corporation was Rs. 500 crore. The Corporation has a paid-up share capital of Rs. 257.95 crore, of which the Central Government contribution was Rs. 217 crore and the remaining amount was contributed by States/UTs.

The scheme of 'micro-financing' has also been introduced in 1998-99 and the same is operated directly through NGOs and SHGs. Of the Ninth Plan allocation of Rs.111 crore for the Corporation, an amount of Rs. 92.26 crore was spent, benefiting 81,695 beneficiaries. All the above-said 5 apex financial institutions, viz. NSFDC, State SCDCs, NSKFDC, NBCFDC, NMDFC which are expected to be working for the economic empowerment of the socially disadvantaged groups, have been strengthened by increasing their Authorised Share Capital during the Ninth Plan. These Corporations, in collaboration with the State Finance and Development Corporations, are expected to work as catalytic agents besides extending both 'forward' and 'backward' linkages of credit and marketing facilities to micro-level agencies to improve the economic status of these groups.

But unfortunately, a critical assessment of the working of all these Corporations over a period of five to ten years has brought forth a most revealing truth that none of them justifies the name of being a Corporation, as they are heavily dependent upon governmental assistance. Generally, these Corporations are expected to become self-reliant over a period of two to three years of their establishment. Instead, they are becoming more and more dependent upon the Government and demanding a hike in the Authorised Share Capital, from time to time, which is not a healthy sign.

For example, the original Authorised Share Capital of Rs. 150 crore for NSFDC has been revised four times to raise it to Rs. 1,000 crore. Further, these Corporations have been maintaining a recovery rate to a maximum of 30 to 50 per cent. A study of the working of all these Corporations during the very first year of the Tenth Plan, with a major objective of introducing necessary reforms has been suggested by the Planning Commission, so as to make them financially viable and become effective instruments in empowering the disadvantaged.

Protective Measures

The Ministry of Social Justice & Empowerment, in its nodal capacity, continued to make special efforts towards ensuring social justice to the weaker sections through enforcement of special legislations and implementation of protective programmes. Towards achieving the major objective of abolishing the practice of untouchability, curtailing/ preventing the incidence of crimes and atrocities committed against SCs and ensuring rehabilitation of the affected victims, efforts were made through effective implementation of the Protection of Civil Rights (PCR) Act, 1955 and the Scheduled Castes and the Scheduled Tribes (Prevention of Atrocities) Act, 1989.

To ensure speedy disposal of cases under the two Acts, 36 Special Courts were set up under the PCR Act and 113 Special Courts under the SC and ST (POA) Act.With a major objective of accomplishing complete eradication of the obnoxious and in-human practice of manual scavenging, the National Scheme of Liberation and Rehabilitation of Scavengers and their Dependents was modified in 1998 to accommodate revised norms and involve NGOs in the efforts made for identification, liberation and rehabilitation of scavengers. Though, complete elimination of the practice of manual scavenging could not be achieved by the end of the Ninth Plan (2002) as targeted, yet around 3.84 lakh out of the 6.53 lakh identified scavengers were rehabilitated, while 1.47 lakh were imparted training to take up alternative vocations.

In addition to these efforts made through special legislation and programmes, the four statutory Commissions viz. i) National Commission for SCs and STs; ii) National Commission for Safai Karamcharis; iii) National Commission for Backward Classes; and iv) National Commission for the Minorities also played a very important role in safeguarding the rights and interests of their target groups. Armed with the powers of a Civil Court, the Commissions investigated individual complaints/ grievances made on-the-spot visits to the areas where the incidence of crimes/atrocities took place and placed the 'Action Taken Reports' before both Houses of Parliament.

The Commission for SCs and STs also played an effective interventionist role in reviewing the progress of the implementation of Special Component Plan (SCP) and Tribal Sub-Plan (TSP) by the Central Ministries/ Departments and the State Governments and also the utilisation of Special Central Assistance (SCA) to SCP and TSP. The outstanding contribution of the Commission during the Plan period was holding national-level consultations with District Development Commissioners/

Collectors to develop a direct district-wise dialogue for receiving the first-hand report on the progress of the implementation of various policies and programmes in improving the status of these Target Groups.

The National Commission for Backward Classes, set up to advise the Government with regard to inclusion of various communities in the List of OBCs and also attend thereto the complaints received, could successfully tender advice to the Government in respect of 1,067 castes/ communities. Out of these, 652 castes were included and 415 were rejected. The Commission also initiated action on completing the task within the available time-frame.

The other achievements include setting up of a Minority Education Cell by the National Commission for Minorities to look after exclusively the problems faced by the Minority Educational Institutions with regard to recognition, allocation, grant-in-aid etc. The National Commission for Safai Karamcharis, set up in 1994, has been playing its role in promoting as well as safeguarding the interests and rights of Safai Karamcharis, besides investigating specific grievances as well as matters relating to implementation of programmes and schemes for the welfare of the Safai Karamcharis. It also has the responsibility of over-seeing the progress of fulfilling the national commitment of Total Eradication of Manual Scavenging.

Implementation of SCP and SCA to SCP for SCs

The two innovative strategies of SCP for SCs and the SCA to SCP have been receiving special attention right from their introduction in 1979-80, as these are the most effective mechanisms to ensure additional flow of funds/ benefits for SCs. SCP demands earmarking of population proportionate funds for the development of SCs from the general development sectors. As per the information available, only 14 Central Ministries/ Departments and

22 States/UTs are adhering to the earmarking of funds for SCs.

SCA to SCP is a Central scheme to extend 100 per cent grant as an additive to strengthen the efforts of the states to fill the critical gaps under the family-based income generation projects, to cater to those SC families living below poverty line. SCA to SCP was enhanced from Rs. 1,125 crore in the Eighth Plan to Rs. 2,092.95 crore in the Ninth Plan, indicating an increase by 86 per cent. Details of the flow of funds, under SCP and SCA to SCP, both at central and state levels during the Ninth Plan are given in Table 1.

Table 1. Flow of Funds under SCP and SCA to SCP for SCs during the Ninth Plan (1997-2002)

(Rs. in Crore)

Item	Outlay	Flow to SCP	Percentage (Col. 3 to Col.2)
(1)	(2)	(3)	(4)
Special Component Plan (SCP)			
- Flow from Central Plan (in respect of 14 Ministries/Departments)	15,478.90	1,646.00	10.63
- Flow from State Plan (in respect of 22 States/UTs)	3,46,717.05	42,308.97	12.20
Special Central Assistance (SCA) to SCP			
- SCA to SCP (Outlay & Release)	2,092.95	2,004.68	95.78

As could be seen from Table 1, funds to the extent of Rs. 1,646.00 crore (10.63 per cent) from 14 Ministries/

Departments at the Central level and funds to the extent of Rs. 42,308.97 crore (12.20 per cent) from 22 States/UTs are flowing to SCP. This indicates that efforts need to be made to improve the implementation of SCP at both the central and state levels to reach the expected level.

A quick review of the earmarking of funds under SCP brings forth certain issues like - while some Ministries/Departments being regulatory in nature are not able to earmark funds for SCP, some others having activities which are non-divisible in nature, are finding it difficult to earmark funds under SCP. In respect of SCA to SCP, it was observed that nonrelease of SCA funds on time by the State Finance Departments to the State/nodal departments of Welfare has been adversely affecting the smooth running of various income-generation programmes that are undertaken for SC families living below the poverty line.

Such delays are not only affecting the beneficiary families but also causing predicament to the nodal department, as they are not able to make full use of the allocated funds, and finally resulting in unspent funds. Often, such unspent SCA funds, as reported, are getting diverted to other purposes leaving the earmarked/ intended purposes unattended to. To look into all the related issues, a Central Standing Tripartite Committee was set up by the Planning Commission in May 1999 with the representatives of the Planning Commission, National Commission for SCs and STs, the nodal Ministry of Social Justice & Empowerment and the concerned Central Ministries/Departments.

The Committee has, so far, reviewed formulations of both SCP and TSP of the 14 Central Ministries/ Departments of Agriculture and Co-operation, Environment and Forest, Urban Development and Poverty Alleviation, Rural Development, Indian System of Medicine and Homeopathy, Non-Conventional Energy

Sources, Water Resources, Public Enterprises, Animal Husbandry & Dairying, Sugar and Edible Oils, Drinking Water Supply, Statistics and Programme Implementation, Food Processing and Power and advised that all the Ministries/Departments should put in their special efforts to revive the otherwise routinised SCP and TSP.

It also suggested that the formulation of SCP and TSP should be right at the plan formulation stage through - identification of schemes and earmarking of funds so that a systematic monitoring of the utilisation of earmarked funds can be planned for. Similar Committees are also coming up at the state level. So far, 6 states viz., Andhra Pradesh, Bihar, Madhya Pradesh, West Bengal, Punjab and Gujarat have set up such Committees. Other States/UTs are also expected to come up soon with such Committees to review the progress of the implementation of SCP, TSP and SCA to SCP and TSP on a continuing basis.

Scheduled Castes

As a result of various affirmative actions, pro-active policies and programmatic interventions put into action by the government, along with the committed efforts of various NGOs, the status of SCs has registered quantifiable improvement during the last five developmental decades. Yet, a lot more needs to be done to fulfil the Constitutional commitment of raising the status of SCs to that of the rest of the population. The gains and gaps, as recorded through various developmental indicators, are detailed below: SC population as a percentage of total population has increased from 14.6 in 1971 to 17.5 in 2001 (Table 2).

Though the decadal growth rate for SCs, estimated to be 30 per cent, was more than the growth rate of 21.3 per cent of the total population in 2001, yet a decline was noticed between 1991 and 2001. The sex ratio of SCs as it stood in 1991 was not only adverse, but also showed a declining trend as it fell from 935 in 1971 to 922 in 1991 (Table 3).

Table 2. Population and Decadal Growth Rate of SCs and Total Population (1971-2001)

(Figures in Million)

Census	Population		Decadal Growth Rate	
	Total	SCs	Total	SCs
(1)	(2)	(3)	(4)	(5)
1971	548.1	80.0 (14.6)	24.8	24.2
1981	683.4	104.7 (15.3)	24.7	30.9
1991	846.3	138.2 (16.5)	23.9	32.0
2001 (Projected)	1027.0	179.7# (17.5)	21.3	30.0 (estimated)

Table 3. Sex Ratio of SCs and Total Population (1971-2001)

Census	Sex Ratio (No. of Females per 1,000 Males) Total Population	SC Population
(1)	(2)	(3)
1971	930	935
1981	934	932
1991	927	922
2001	933	Not yet available

In fact, the sex ratio of SCs, which held a better status than that of the total population in 1971, suddenly took a turn to worse in 1981 and continued with the same tempo. This, as a gender concern, needs to be looked into. Higher mortality amongst females and their limited access to health and family welfare services could be attributed to the causes of this adverse sex ratio. However, this is not an exception to SCs alone, but a common feature in respect of general population also.

Educational Status

Education, being the most important instrument for empowering weaker sections of the society, every effort is being made to improve the educational status of SCs on priority basis. Between 1971 and 1991, the literacy rate of SCs increased by 2.6 times, while that of total population increased by 1.8 times (Table 4). However, the gap between the literacy rates of SCs and of the total population continued during the two decades between 1971 and 1991 almost at the same level of 14 per cent and above, but with slight variations.

Table 4. Literacy Rates of SCs and Total Population (1971-2001)

(in per cent)

Category	1971	1981	1991	2001
(1)	(2)	(3)	(4)	(5)
Total Population	29.45	36.23	52.21	65.38
Scheduled Castes	14.67	21.38	37.41	Not yet
Gap between SCs and Total Population	14.78	14.85	14.80	available

Female literacy, which is another important indicator in the field of education, reveals that the situation in respect of SC females was worse with 6.44 per cent when compared to the total population of 18.69 per cent in 1971. No doubt, SC females made a very good progress in increasing their literacy rate almost by fourfolds i.e. from 6.44 per cent in 1971 to 23.76 per cent in 1991, when compared to the two times progress made by the total population, but it still continues to be very low (Table 5). Similarly, the gap between the literacy rates of SC females and that of the total females has widened from 12.25 per cent in 1971 to 18.92 per cent in 1981 and declined to 15.53 per cent in 1991.

Table 5

Category	1971	1981	1991	2001
(1)	(2)	(3)	(4)	(5)
Total Population	18.69	29.85	39.29	54.16
Scheduled Castes	6.44	10.93	23.76	Not yet available
Gap between Female litracy of SCs and Total Population	12.25	18.92	15.53	

The Gross Enrolment Ratios (GER) of SC boys and girls at the primary level not only declined over 1990-91 to 1999-2000, but they were also lower than those for the total population in 1999-2000 (Table 6). At the middle level, good pace of progress was maintained by the SCs, especially by the SC girls. In fact, GERs of both SC boys and girls were higher than those for total population, at the middle level in 1999-2000.

Table 6. Gross Enrolment Ratios of SCs and Total Population (1990-91 to 1999-2000)

	Year	1990-91		1999-2000	
	Classes	I to V	I to VIII	I to V	I to VIII
	(1)	(2)	(3)	(4)	(5)
Total Population*	Total	100.1	62.1	94.9	58.8
	Boys	114.0	76.6	104.1	67.2
	Girls	85.5	47.8	85.2	49.7
Scheduled	Total	102.2	47.7	92.4	62.5

Castes	Boys	122.7	61.4	103.6	73.6
	Girls	80.6	33.3	80.5	50.3
GAP	Total	(+) 2.1	(-) 14.4	(-) 2.5	(+) 3.7
	Boys	(+) 8.7	(-) 15.2	(-) 0.5	(+) 6.4
	Girls	(-) 4.9	(-) 14.5	(-) 4.7	(+) 0.6

The drop-out rate is another crucial indicator in the field of educational development. The figures are still very high - 44.27 in classes I to V; 63.58 in classes I to VIII; and 76.63 in classes I to X in 1998-99 (Table 7). This indicates clearly that the problem gets worse at the higher levels of schooling. However, an encouraging sign is the reduction in the gap between the drop-out rates of the total population and SCs at all levels between 1990-91 and 1998-99.

Table 7. Drop-Out Rates amongst SCs and Total Population (1990-91 and 1998-99)

(in per cent)

Category	Classes (I-V)		Classes (I-VIII)		Classes (I-X)	
	1990-91	1998-99	1990-91	1998-99	1990-9	1998-99
(1)	(2)	(3)	(4)	(5)	(6)	(7)
Total*	42.60	39.74	60.90	56.82	71.34	67.44
SCs	49.40	44.27	72.09	63.58	80.58	76.63
GAP	6.80	4.53	11.19	6.76	9.24	9.19

Economic Status

Poverty alleviation programmes put into action both in rural and urban areas since the 1980s have not only helped the poor people to rise above the poverty line, but also brought down the poverty rates quite effectively, as shown at Table 8.

The rate of decline in respect of the percentage of SCs living below the poverty line was marginally higher than that of the total population between 1993-94 and 1999-2000. The gap between the total population and the SCs also decreased during the same period in both urban and rural areas. However, the incidence of poverty amongst SCs still continues to be very high with 36.25 per cent in rural areas and 38.47 per cent in urban areas, when compared to 27.09 and 23.62 per cent respectively, in respect of total population in 1999-2000 (Table 8). This is primarily due to the fact that a large number of SCs who are living below the poverty line are landless with no productive assets and with no access to sustainable employment and minimum wages. The women belonging to these Groups suffer even worse because of the added disadvantage of being denied of equal and minimum wages.

Table 8. Population Living Below Poverty Line (1993-94 and 1999-2000)

(in per cent)

Category	1993-94		1999-2000		Percentage Decrease (1993-94 to 1999-2000)	
	Rural	Urban	Rural	Urban	Rural	Urban
(1)	(2)	(3)	(4)	(5)	(6)	(7)
Total	37.27	32.38	27.09	23.62	(-) 10.18	(-) 10.04
SCs	48.11	49.48	36.25	38.47	(-) 11.86	(-) 11.01
GAP	10.84	15.82	9.16	14.85	(-) 1.68	(-) 0.97

Participation in Decision-Making

Administration

Participation of SCs in decision-making is a positive indicator of progress made by them. The two Tables 9 reflect the representation of SCs in the All India Services of the Indian Administrative Service (IAS), Indian Police Service (IPS) and Indian Forest Service (IFS) as well as Other categories:

Representation of SCs in All India Services of IAS, IPS and IFS is not very encouraging, as they represent 10.6 per cent of the total in the IAS, 12.4 per cent in the IPS and 11.5 per cent in the IFS in 2000 which is still below their expected level (Table 9). Although, the percentage of SCs in IAS and IPS declined between 1996 and 2000, yet the actual number has increased over the same period.

Table 9. Representation of SCs in the All India Services during 1996 and 2000

Category	IAS		IPS		IFS	
	1996	2000	1996	2000	1996	2000
(1)	(2)	(3)	(4)	(5)	(6)	(7)
Total	5047	5519	2947	3301	2305	2557
SCs	546	548	381	408	261	295
	(10.8)	(10.6)	(12.9)	(12.4)	(11.3)	(11.5)

The rise in the total representation of SCs in Central Government Services covering A to D Groups from 13.66 per cent in 1974 to 16.70 per cent in 1999, is marginally higher than their share in the total population. Although, their representation has shown an increasing trend from 3.25 per cent in 1974 to 11.29 per cent in 1999 in Group A Services, though not the expected level, it does reflect the impact of various affirmative measures taken for bringing them into the mainstream.

Political

Affirmative discrimination through reservation for SCs in the Lok Sabha, State Legislative Assemblies and in the Panchayati Raj Institutions (PRIs) has established the growing strength of SCs not only in terms of their participation in the democratic processes of the country since independence, but also their increasing representation in the political decisionmaking.

The representation of SCs in the political decision-making institutions at various levels has been quite impressive, though yet to receive their due share in PRIs, State Legislative Assemblies and Lok Sabha (Table 10). Further, while in the PRIs, the share of SCs stood at 14.3 per cent in 2001, their share in State Legislative Assemblies was 13.8 per cent in 2000 and 14.5 per cent in the Lok Sabha in 1999. The representation of SCs in the Central Council of Ministers has increased marginally in absolute numbers from 6 to 7 during the period between 1991 and 1999. However, their representation as a percentage to the total has declined from 10.5 per cent to 9.5 per cent over the same period. Of the 7 SCs in the Central Council of Ministers in 1999, 3 are of Cabinet rank and 4 are Ministers of State.

Table 10. Representation of SCs in the Central Council of Ministers (1991 & 1999)

Year	SCs	General	Total
(1)	(2)	(3)	(4)
1991	6	51	57
	(10.5)		
1999	7	67	74
	(9.5)		

Other backward classes

As already explained in the very beginning of this Chapter, no authentic data is available even about the size of the population of OBCs, leave aside on the other aspects of development to assess their status. However, OBCs by profession, being small cultivators, agricultural labourers, artisans and also being engaged in weaving, fishing, construction work etc. and these occupations being common to SCs and OBCs, the status of OBCs cannot be treated as very much different from that of SCs.

Minorities

Even in the case of Minorities, nonavailability of authentic data makes it difficult to assess their socio-economic status. Therefore, one has to depend upon the information generated either by occasional surveys or by various research studies. Based on the data emerging through a survey conducted by the National Council for Applied Economic Research (NCAER), New Delhi in 1994 covering 33,230 rural households in 16 states, Muslims have been identified as backward, both educationally and economically, when compared to the other Minority Groups. However, as the sample of the Survey is so very limited, the findings/conclusions of the Survey cannot be taken as a true reflection of the national profile of the Minorities.

Approach to the Tenth Plan

The long-drawn process of empowering the socially and economically Disadvantaged Groups launched during the Ninth Plan has, no doubt, enabled them to develop their capacities and capabilities to be the active partners and partakers of the country's development, rather than continuing as passive recipients of various developmental benefits. Therefore, the very process of empowering these Disadvantaged Groups, viz. SCs, OBCs and Minorities will continue as the major approach in the Tenth Plan and beyond till the Constitutional commitment of raising their status to that of the rest of the society is fulfilled.

The first step in this direction will be to initiate action with a holistic approach to alter the harsh conditions in which these Groups live and work so as to accomplish all round development of these weaker sections with an effective intersectoral co-ordination inputs from both the governmental and non-governmental organisations. Improvement in the socio-economic conditions of these vulnerable groups will be made possible only by removing the disparities and eliminating exploitation and suppression. To this effect, due weightage and priority will be given to programmes catering to educational and economic development by taking into consideration the varying status of each target group viz. SCs, OBCs and Minorities.

Also, every effort will be made to reach the developmental benefits to all the needy persons belonging to these Groups and thus ensure equitable distribution and growth with social justice. In these efforts, the major focus will be to accomplish the task of providing basic needs to one and all as an essential measure for realizing empowerment amongst these weaker sections. Accordingly, the fulfilment of basic needs viz. food and nutrition, safe drinking water, primary health care, primary education, shelter, sanitation, good environment etc. becomes a priority. To this effect, special attention will, therefore, be paid to attend to the problems of resettlement and rehabilitation of the large influx of rural population belonging to the Socially Disadvantaged Groups congregating into urban slums.

Efforts will, therefore, be made through the on-going programme of Pradhan Mantri Gramodaya Yojana to ensure that the above said basic minimum services reach every habitation with concentration of these groups. Further, while formulating/implementing programmes for these Groups, the Tenth Plan will strive to ensure 'People-Centred Development' and 'People's Participation' with effective involvement of PRIs in pursuance of the

73rd and 74t h Constitutional Amendments. Immediate steps will also be taken for the devolution of financial as well as administrative powers to PRIs and Local Bodies so that these marginalised groups will get opportunity to participate in the formulation of the need-based programmes, as well as in their effective implementation, supervision and monitoring.

This will not only go a long way in empowering these Groups, but will also ensure that implementation of various developmental programmes is taken care of in the true sense of decentralised planning. While SCs, OBCs and Minorities, in general, occupy a lower status in the society, their women and children, especially the girl child represent the weakest link. Though there has been a perceptible improvement in the overall situation of these women, yet the development indicators that reflect their status imply that they are the most deprived and discriminated, when compared to their counterpart women belonging to other communities. While taking note of their plight, the Tenth Plan proposes to adopt a comprehensive strategy towards ensuring their protection, welfare, development and empowerment through extending special educational, health, nutrition, employment, legal and other services.

The nodal Ministry of Social Justice & Empowerment, in collaboration with the Department of Women and Child Development, will ensure that SC women receive their rightful share, both funds and benefits, from all the other developmental sectors under the Women's Component Plan. While the above paragraphs outline the general approach towards empowering the Socially Disadvantaged Groups during the Tenth Plan, details of the Group-wise strategy in achieving the much wanted - 'Social Empowerment' through removal of the still existing inequalities, disparities and other persisting problems; 'Economic

Empowerment' through various employment-cum-income generation activities with an ultimate objective of making them economically independent and selfreliant; and 'Social Justice' through elimination of all types of discrimination against these Groups with the strength and support of legislative measures, awareness generation and change in the mind-set of the people, are discussed below:

I. Social Empowerment

Scheduled Castes

Education being the best means not only to empower the disadvantaged, but also to provide the essential base for all developmental pursuits, the Tenth Plan will work out special effective interventions to 'reach the un-reached' and thus fill the existing gaps between the SCs and the general population, with a focus on SC women and the girl children. All the efforts in this direction will, therefore, take into consideration the scenario that has emerged i.e. on the one hand, there exists a definite improvement in the literacy rates of SCs and on the other, there persists a gap between the literacy rates of SCs and the general population, even till today.

Further, the Tenth Plan will endeavour to improve the educational status of SCs on a timebound basis, in close collaboration with the Department of Elementary Education, as part of the total commitment of making the country fully literate by the year 2007. The Tenth Plan will make special efforts to fulfil this commitment through universalisation of elementary education with a special focus on low-literacy pockets and on the educationally backward SCs, whose literacy rates are very low compared to the rest of the population. The on-going programmes of the Department of Elementary Education viz. Sarva Shiksha Abhiyan, DPEP, Shiksha

Karmi, NFE, Mid-Day Meals etc. are going to play a major role in this endeavour.

In fact, the recent directive of the Supreme Court to treat education as a fundamental right imposes an ultimatum on the Tenth Plan to act rigorously to improve the educational status of SCs and thus accomplish social empowerment. The first step in this direction will be to arrest the problem of school drop-outs, and improve enrolment/retention rates by ensuring easy access; and provision of adequate support facilities like hostels, crèches and special incentives to poor students like scholarships, free books, free uniforms, transport charges, besides compensation to families etc.

Here the earlier initiatives of starting crèches/Anganwadis within the school campus or near to the school will be revived to ensure that the girl children are not deprived of education, while substituting for their mothers when the latter go out to work. To this effect, the scheme of Balika Samriddhi Yojana, an exclusive programme for girl children living below the poverty line and the much wanted nutritional support through the popular scheme of Mid-Day Meals will be expanded/universalised to improve both enrolment/retention rates.

Further, steps will also be taken to ensure provision of quality education to equip the educationally backward SCs to enhance their employment prospects with competitive ability and thus mitigate the problems of their marginalisation and deprivation in the employment market. Along with the general education, efforts will also be made to vocationalise education both at the middle and high school levels to enable SC students to enhance their technical and productive capabilities in those vocations that have a direct bearing/relevance to their local needs and market demands. To this effect, job-oriented condensed courses of education and training will be given priority. In all these efforts, the ultimate objective will be to fulfil the Tenth Plan commitment of minimising the gap between the educational status of SCs and that of the general population.

Other backward classes

The new interventions launched during the Ninth Plan for improving the educational status of OBCs, viz. scholarships for both post-matric and pre-matric students and hostels for OBC students, will continue with much larger coverage to enlarge the accessibility to the otherwise educationally backward OBCs. The special programmes of National Literacy Mission and Shiksha Karmi run by the Department of Elementary Education will also take care of the needs and interests of OBCs by extending a special focus as well as the coverage. Steps will also be taken not only to bring about qualitative improvement in the education for OBCs, but will also be enriched through adding vocational education/ training which is of great functional utility/ value and thus prevent educational wastage.

To this effect, the Tenth Plan will make special efforts to expand the on-going schemes and thus extend easy accessibility to OBC students through the existing network of the Ministry of Labour viz. National Vocational Training Institute, Regional Vocational Training Institutes, Industrial Training Institutes and Craft Training Centres spread all over the country. The Tenth Plan will extend priority attention to OBC women and girl children in all the on-going educational and training programmes.

Minorities

Minorities who constitute a sizeable and potential population to contribute to the country's development process will be given prominence and priority in the Tenth Plan through a comprehensive approach towards their educational development, and economic prosperity by maximizing their productive potentialities in various sectors with a special focus on their traditional artisanship.

As the crucial drawback in the development of Minorities, especially Muslims, primarily lies in their educational backwardness, exclusive efforts in the Tenth Plan will be made to promote educational development of Muslims, especially of their women and girl children by modernising and mainstreaming their traditional education system and institutions viz. Madarsas, through adopting syllabi being followed in the regular education system.

To inculcate a sense of security and prevent marginalisation and isolation of Minorities, both protective and promotional measures as per the Constitutional provisions in favour of Minorities, will be taken in educational, economic and legislative spheres. To accomplish their socioeconomic upliftment and mainstreaming, steps will be taken to generate responsive awareness amongst the civil society and thus create an enabling/conducive atmosphere for the advancement of the Minorities.

To this effect, involvement of the Minorities, especially their women, in the grassroot level institutions will be encouraged as the best means towards empowering them. Special attention will also be paid to the backward Minority concentrated pockets/ areas in providing basic amenities/services viz. primary education, health, nutrition, safe drinking water, sanitation etc. The Tenth Plan will also ensure effective implementation of the 15-Point Programme which is a comprehensive package of both protective and developmental measures towards improving the status of Minorities.

II. Economic Empowerment

Scheduled Castes

Towards the economic upliftment of SCs, the Tenth Plan will prioritise those activities that ensure employment and income generation which can provide them sustainable income to meet their basic needs. Recognising their traditional ability and skills in the agriculture production, efforts will be made not only to endow every landless SC family with a minimum piece of land with ownership rights but also to maximise their productive capacities through upgradation of their skills, modernisation of methods and equipment and supply of seeds and pesticides etc.

Also, the State Departments will be persuaded to ensure that irrigation facilities are extended to the small land holdings of SC farmers, collectively so as to reduce the relative costs. Special legislative measures will also be taken to ensure payment of minimum wages and equal wages for women, with no gender discrimination, especially in the informal/un-organised sector.

The on-going efforts made for uplifting SCs above the poverty line will be further intensified/ expanded, with an ultimate objective of enhancing their income levels at a higher pace so that they could be brought above the poverty line on a priority basis. To this effect, all the poverty alleviation programmes would be reinvigorated and expanded to make a better impact on the economic conditions of SCs leading to qualitative betterment in their overall living conditions. Thus, the strategy in the Tenth Plan will be to implement the on-going nation-wide poverty alleviation programmes, with enriched components, best suited to the specific needs and poverty situations of the SCs. This will include organising landless and agricultural labourers to constitute the largest occupational segments amongst SCs on the pattern of swarozgaris of the SGSY with special focus on women.

In the changing economic scenario wherein the private sector is being consciously promoted to take up all production and commercial activities and the role of government sector is getting restricted to core activities, the Tenth Plan will endeavour to reorient SCs to face the challenges arising out of the inevitable economic reforms. Further, as the services sector today represents the fastest growing sector of the economy whose contribution is going to increase manifold in providing new employment opportunities in the coming years, the strategy to be adopted for empowering SCs will be in consonance with this changing phenomenon.

With the globalisation and liberalisation of economy, new opportunities and avenues, both at the national and international levels, are being opened up substantially. The Tenth Plan will, therefore, endeavour to, in collaboration with the concerned Ministries/ Departments, equip SCs with technical knowledge and ability to cope with the upcoming trades and trends in the employment market. Interventions with appropriate training, technology, capacity-building, development of entrepreneurship, either individually or collectively through formation of Co-operatives/Self-Help Groups (SHGs) along with both 'forward and backward' linkages will be made to produce quality goods, as per the demand, and thus exploit the market to the extent possible.

To this end, the Tenth Plan will initiate action to tie up with the concerned Ministries dealing with agriculture, fisheries, dairying, animal husbandry, handlooms and handicrafts to open up avenues for exports. The exclusive Financial Institution working for the economic empowerment of SCs viz. the NSFDC and State-level Corporations, will be geared to function as catalytic agents for accomplishing economic development of respective weaker sections by making them self-reliant and selfsustaining mechanisms.

For this purpose, the functioning of this Apex Corporation will be reviewed and necessary reforms be brought into with the strength of professional expertise in marketing and business management to ensure that this exclusive Corporation proves its worth as an effective financial institution in improving the economic status of SCs. Simultaneous efforts will also be made to ensure effective earmarking and utilisation of funds under the special strategy of SCP, both at the central and state levels, besides the funds released under SCA to SCP to ensure optimum benefit to improve the economic status of SCs through family-oriented income-generation activities.

Special efforts will also be made by both Central and State Standing Tripartite Committees (CSSTC) to impress upon those Ministries/Departments, which are not earmarking funds, under SCP in the name of nondivisibility of the programmes of their Ministries/ Departments to do the needful. While the nodal Ministry of Social Justice & Empowerment will keep a close vigil on the utilisation of these special funds, the on-going reviews at the Centre both by the CSSTC and the National Commission for SCs and STs will continue on a regular basis to assess how effective are these instruments in supplementing/ complementing the efforts of the nodal Ministry in empowering these disadvantaged groups economically.

Other backward classes

Recognising the productive potential of the OBCs who form the major workforce, the strategy for the development of OBCs in the Tenth Plan will be to optimise their productive and technical abilities, so that they can develop the formidable human resource of the country. Thus, efforts will be made for the socio-economic development of OBCs, as a strategic input for building up human resources of the country.

As OBCs engaged in the primary sector also depend upon a broad spectrum of occupations/ artisanship and provide a variety of services/ products for consumption of the society, efforts of the Tenth Plan will be to encourage those productive sectors that the OBCs are engaged in, especially by extending necessary support including skill upgradation, capacity building, training, market linkages, credit support etc. so as to accomplish betterment in their economic status.

Also, as a majority of OBCs depend upon agriculture, OBC farmers will be encouraged and supported to adopt innovative land- based activities viz., the cultivation of medicinal plants, horticulture, commercial crops etc. with a major objective to bring them above the level of their subsistence economy and rescue them from the risks and uncertainties involved in agricultural practices. Some of the OBC communities, especially those living in rural areas, depend upon the traditional occupations/artisanship viz. fishing, stone crushing, tailoring, weaving, scavenging, carpentry, pottery, blacksmithy, etc. and are languishing in the worst forms of social and economic backwardness.

Efforts in the Tenth Plan will, therefore, be to encourage occupational mobility for those OBCs, especially the youth, who intend to discontinue their traditional occupations, by providing facilities for appropriate educational and vocational training in modern and up-coming technologies, supplemented with financial and other assistance to enable them to enter successfully into new avenues.

As the New Economic Policy has opened up vast markets abroad for Indian exports, especially in the field of software industry and other Service Sector Enterprises leading to an explosion in job and business opportunities, the Tenth Plan will concentrate on intensifying various training programmes through careful planning to equip these disadvantaged categories to enable them to capitalise on the emerging employment opportunities. In addition, efforts will also be made within the country to open up opportunities for small entrepreneurial ventures to increase the reach of the weaker sections.

Towards ensuring economic development of OBCs involved in the traditional occupations, the Tenth Plan will have a special commitment of ensuring their capacity building through skill upgradation, training and entrepreneurial development programmes. The strategy of the Tenth Plan will, therefore, be to help/encourage the artisans belonging to these weaker sections to trigger both horizontal and vertical mobility in their occupations. Further, a gradual infusion of technology will be planned for, especially in the handlooms and handicrafts sectors, so that the value is added to the goods produced for effective marketing, both in the national and international markets. In these efforts, NBCFDC is going to play a very major role in tying up both backward and forward linkages of credit and marketing.

Minorities

As a sizeable population of the Minority communities is engaged in the traditional arts and crafts like handlooms, handicrafts, chikan work, zari work, lace making, glass work, metal works etc. and continue to depend upon these low-paid traditional artisanship for their livelihood, the Tenth Plan will give priority to modernize the technologies especially in the much needed handloom sector to add value to their produce by extending appropriate support in terms of vocational training in the up-coming technologies, skill upgradation, credit facilities etc. Special efforts will also be made to encourage exportoriented handicrafts in view of their increasing demand outside the country. NMDFC will be encouraged to extend financial and other technical support like provision of machinery, expertise, training, market linkages etc.

Efforts will also be made to provide technical and vocational education/training facilities to the Minority artisans and craftsmen focusing on their women and girl children engaged in such pursuits. Also, to preserve their traditional skills, they will be encouraged to form into SHGs/Cooperatives for which financial assistance will be extended along with credit and marketing services. The on-going economic reforms of globalisation, liberalization and privatisation, resulting in the emergence of new opportunities at the national and international levels will be exploited for the economic benefit of the Minorities.

Towards this end, modernisation of traditional education, imparting of vocational and technical education, introduction of appropriate technology, and development of entrepreneurship along with necessary financial support will be adopted as one of the key strategies for their economic development during the Tenth Plan.

Effective implementation of the existing schemes and programmes for the welfare and development of Minorities and for integrating them into the national mainstream, both economically and socially will be given priority attention in the Tenth Plan. NMDFC will be encouraged to promote self-employment activities amongst the various minority groups and to provide upgraded/ entrepreneurial technical skills, especially focusing on the development of Minority viz. women, traditional artisans and other occupational groups.

III. Social Justice

A conscious shift in the name and role of the nodal Ministry from 'Welfare' to 'Social Justice and Empowerment' in 1998 is not only to re-affirm the governmental commitment of ensuring social justice, but also to extend a focused attention to these Groups. Affirmative action and legislative measures being the most powerful instruments to ensure social justice to the Disadvantaged Groups, the Government renews its earlier commitment of instituting a 'National Charter for Social Justice' based on the principles of social harmony with social and gender justice and necessary legal measures to protect their interests. To this effect, implementation of the reservation policy both in the educational institutions and services for SCs, and in services for OBCs will be strictly adhered to by filling up all the reserved posts promptly.

Arrangements will also be made simultaneously for quick judicial disposals of complaints and grievances in matters related thereof. As the most inhuman practice of carrying the night soil manually continues to be a matter of national concern, the Tenth Plan will embark upon a nation-wide programme for total eradication of manual scavenging on a time-bound basis by 2007. To this effect, the Tenth Plan will emphasise preparation of State-specific Plans of Action to initiate time-bound programmes in respect of - conversion of dry latrines into wet ones; identification of scavengers; wean them away from this profession; and rehabilitate them with training and alternative jobs; keep a follow-up of the rehabilitated persons; and bring forth an effective coordination between the Welfare Departments of the States and the Local Bodies.

In these national endeavours, the National Commission for Safai Karamcharis is going to play a lead role. Taking note of the urgent need for upholding the Civil Rights on the one hand and preventing/curbing the persistent problems of social discrimination, exploitation, untouchability, and atrocities against these disadvantaged groups, on the other, the Tenth Plan will initiate collaborative efforts with all the concerned for effective implementation of the Indian Penal Code, 1860 and the other two Special Legislations viz. the PCR Act, 1955 and the SC & ST (Prevention of Atrocities) Act, 1989. To this effect, efforts will also be made to prepare state /district-specific Programmes of Action ensuring preventive, investigative and rehabilitative measures in those districts/areas where the incidence of crime/ atrocities/ violence against these weaker sections is high.

Measures will also be undertaken to ensure that adequate number of Special/ Mobile Courts are set up with adequate staff in each district to provide both speedy and on-the-spot settlement/redressal of grievances. Further, the problem relating to the practice of untouchability which is still in vogue in certain pockets will be addressed squarely towards total elimination of the same from the face of the society.

As an important measure of social justice, special efforts will be made to extend timely and adequate financial support, as per the provisions, to compensate/ rehabilitate the victims. Simultaneously, efforts will also be made to develop a community-based defence mechanism by empowering the institutions of local governance and NGOs. As part of these, a few selected local NGOs will also be identified to help assist the victims besides acting as the authorised informants to the Enforcement Authorities.

Simultaneously, the Tenth Plan will also endeavour to reinforce the implementation of both the mechanisms viz. SCP for SCs and SCA to SCP which was launched specially in support of social justice to ensure that adequate funds flow for the development of SCs through various sources. While SCP ensures that additional funds, in proportion to the population of SCs, are earmarked for implementation of various programmes for their development, the SCA to SCP extends additional funds to fill the critical gaps in the family-based income-generation activities being implemented under State SCP.

Taking note of the fact that the implementation of these mechanisms is becoming routinised, the Tenth Plan will activate all the concerned, especially the Central Tripartite Committee as well as the nodal Ministry of Social Justice & Empowerment and the State Planning and Welfare Departments to keep continuous monitoring towards more effective implementation of these two mechanisms.

In this chapter, the State Governments which are yet to set up State Tripartite Committees will be involved to initiate necessary action for setting up of these Committees and start the detailed reviews with regard to earmarking of funds under SCP and the utilization of SCA to SCP. Also, the Tenth Plan will take special measures to ensure effective implementation and monitoring of the other two Special Mechanisms viz. the '20-Point Programme' (Point 11-A) for ensuring Social Justice to SCs and the '15-Point Programme' for protection and development of Minorities. Thus, the Tenth Plan will ensure that these special mechanisms justify the purpose for which they were launched by keeping a special vigil on the effectiveness of their implementation.

Further, the Tenth Plan will invoke all the four statutory Commissions viz. National Commission for SCs and STs, National Commission for OBCs, National

Commission for Minorities and National Commission for Safai Karamcharis to make a detailed review of their work since their inception and revitalise themselves to be able to play their role as Custodians and Public Defenders and thus, ensure Social Justice to the deprived lot.

Special efforts will be made to put into action simultaneously the three-pronged strategy of 'Awareness Generation, Conscientisation and Sensitisation', towards achieving a holistic impact. The first being awareness generation, efforts will be made to change the mind-set and the attitudes of the people towards these Groups as the same is very crucial in creating an enabling environment for empowering them.

To this effect, awareness generation programmes/ special campaigns will be taken up on a continuing basis all over the country, especially in rural areas by involving effectively both the governmental and the non-governmental organisations and the media towards erasing the longstanding social biases/stigmas like untouchability and thus create the feeling of all being equal.

The second being conscientisation of the target groups, simultaneous efforts will be made to make the target groups conscious of their own rights, privileges and the governmental support available for them besides making them realise their own potentials to be selfconfident and self-reliant. The third being sensitising both officials and non-officials, special training programmes, both pre-service and in-service, will be undertaken from time to time to sensitise all those working for these Groups so that they can work with right perspectives in handling/meeting the special needs and problems of these marginalised groups and thus ensure social justice.

To encourage/reward those officials and non-officials, who are working for the good of these deprived lot by living in the most backward areas, efforts will be made to impress upon the State Governments the urgent need to revive the earlier practice of extending incentives, both in kind and cash.

3

Labour Welfare and Social Security

The productivity of labour is an essential condition for the prosperity of enterprises and the well being of the workers and their families. While the production facilities at workplace and the remuneration are important, attitudes towards work, and the value placed by the society on dignity of labour are equally important in influencing the productivity of labour.

The planning process supports the attainment of economic and social objectives in the labour sector through a set of strategies. The supply of labour is kept in tune with demand through skill development and vocational training. Appropriate conditions at work are ensured by measures taken to promote safety at the workplace and minimising occupational hazards. A reasonable return on labour is facilitated by labour laws that regulate payment of wages and provision of social security to workers.

Situations where the supply of labour exceeds demand by a huge margin can lead to highly exploitative forms of work. Therefore, an effective implementation of the existing regulations relating to prohibition of bonded (forced) labour and child labour and monitoring the conditions of migrant workers is required.

Tenth Plan Objectives

The present infrastructure for improving labour productivity and for ensuring the welfare of workers covers only a very small segment of the labour force. The objective of Tenth Plan will be to increase the coverage of the labour market institutions. The essential condition for this is the provision of gainful employment to the entire labour force.

However, certain recent trends make the attainment of these objectives a more challenging task. The growth of population in the working age group is at a substantially higher pace than that of the average population. Agriculture used to provide employment to a major part of the workforce. However, the number of workers deployed in agriculture cropping activities has not increased in recent years and it has even declined in certain parts of the country. The pace of growth of jobs in the organised sector has slowed down primarily because number of jobs in the public sector has reduced and employment elasticity in the private sector has decreased significantly.

The economic policy in general, and labour policy in particular, must facilitate the opening up of new employment avenues. In agriculture and related sectors, there is need to create more employment opportunities in horticulture, animal husbandry, poultry, and development of watersheds. However, the nonagricultural sectors of the economy will have to absorb the bulk of the increase in labour force. The labour sector has to focus at those kinds of establishments where much of the labour finds work.

Labour Policy and the Smaller Establishments

The Economic Census enumerates economic activities other than those which are purely for self-consumption and agricultural crop production. It identifies two types of enterprises that operate in such economic activities - the own account enterprises (OAE), which operate without any hired workers and establishments which hire workers. Labour regulations apply to the second category.

Ninety-five per cent of establishments employ less than 20 workers, and 60 per cent of the workers serve in such establishments. (Tables 1 and 2). In order to reach the bulk of the workers, labour policies and programmes have to focus on the requirements of the small establishments. This is in contrast to the situation in recent years, where the large enterprises and their workers have been the focus of labour policy.

Table 1. Distribution of establishments by employment size class

Employment size1 establishments	Agricultural establishments	Non agricultural
1-5	86.4	81.3
6-19	12.7	15.4
20-99	0.8	3.1
100-499	-	0.1
Above500	-	-
All establishments	100.0	100.0
No. of establishments (thousand)	(371.9)	(8,601.2)

Development of Vocational Skills

One of the important determinants of labour productivity is the working skills of the worker. Enterprises will be able to absorb the new entrants to labour market only if they have the requisite training. Surveys have revealed that only about 5 per cent of those in 20 to 24 year age group had any kind of technical education, in contrast to the situation in several developing countries. On the other hand, education levels have improved. Fifty-one per cent of those in 20 to 24 age group now have middle school level or higher education. With education becoming compulsory for those in the 6-14 age group, this number is set to increase in the future. If the youth do not have the working skills required by the employers, the incidence of unemployment among the educated youth will increase.

Table 2. Distribution of workers by employment size class of establishments

Employment size1	Agricultural establishments	Non agricultural establishments
1-5	61.4	35.6
6-19	27.9	24.3
20-99	7.4	18.3
100-499	2.7	10.9
Above 500	0.6	10.9
All establishments	100.0	100.0
No. of workers1	(1.39)	(49.66)[2]

Projections of Increase in Labour force indicate that 8-10 million new entrants are required to be trained each year during the Tenth Plan period. Against this, the vocational training/ technical/ professional education sector has a capacity of only 2-2.3 million. The resultant large gap is not entirely due to a shortage in the availability of training infrastructure.

In some training establishments, the enrolment is much below the capacity and dropout rate in training institutes is significant in certain instances. So a part of the gap can be attributed to a lack of demand for vocational training, since the youth may not find the training at the vocational training institute enhances their chances of finding jobs. There is a mismatch between the training facilities available and the skills that employers require. The factors which suppress the demand for vocational traininghave to be addressed. In addition, new ways of generating resources to expand the capacity for training have to be found so that the training system can absorb the large number of new entrants to the labour force. A reform of the vocational training system is, therefore, required.

Reform of the Vocational Training System

The objective of providing skills to all entrants to the labour force will have to be fulfilled by initiatives that (i) increase the demand for training; and (ii) increase the capacity for training. Thus, the process of reform will address both the factors that influence demand for vocational training and the factors that influence supply. So far, the main thrust of Government policies has been on augmenting the supply capacity. Since the factors that restrain the demand did not receive adequate attention, greater returns are expected, in the near future, from the initiatives that increase the demand for vocational training.

Demand For Vocational Training: The demand for vocational training comes from the returns to the trainee in the form of a job and better income and returns to the employer by way of a higher output from a trained worker. If the income expectations of workers exceed the output realised by the employer, the demand for training cannot be sustained, let alone be increased. Hence, the quality of training should be of a standard that the employer expects. On the other hand, if the expectation from training is to get a job in the Government or public sector, which are not expanding much, no useful purpose will be served by acquiring such training.

Improving Linkage Of Training

Employment prospects of trained manpower can increase if the employer has a say in imparting training. In the Ninth Plan, industry-institute interaction was initiated in Industrial Training Institutes (ITIs), whereby Institute Management Committees (IMC) were set up under the leadership of a local employer/ industrialist. However, the IMC has been set up only at 33 ITIs. There has been no such effort outside the labour sector. In the Tenth Plan, State Governments will be encouraged to cover practically all the training institutes by the IMC mode of management. Industries/employerswhich require training for new recruits will get priority in allotment of seats in training institutes.

Though the bulk of the employment opportunities arise in the small establishments, these enterprises do not have an adequate role in the formulation of a policy for training and its implementation. Such involvement can be meaningful only at the local level rather than at the state or national level. The formulation of a training policy in Tenth Plan will give priority to the needs of local small employers.

Apprenticeships in establishments lead to better job prospects than the training based in the institute classroom. The Apprenticeship Training Scheme under the Apprentices Act, 1961 has remained confined to large establishments, especially those in the public sector. Small employers have not been a significant part of the scheme. In the Tenth Plan, the Apprenticeship Training Schemewill be modified keeping the small employers in mind. Payment of stipend should not be made mandatory for small employers.Absorption of apprentice trainees by the establishment to which they are attached should be voluntary.

There is a social divide between those who opt for vocational training after completing schooland those who enter the higher technical/ professional/medical education stream. In the entry requirements for higher applied education, vocational training and even vocational experience should be considered as fulfillment of some part of the requirement of basic education. Entry criteria to higher-level institutions should give higher priority to those coming out of vocational training establishments over those who join after basic and general education in schools.

Thus, the higher applied education streams should be vertically integrated with the training institutes that provide training in industrial trades, medical diagnostics, commercial practice, tailoring, cooking, travel services, accounting, financial services, insurance services etc. This requires closer interaction between the authorities that regulate higher applied education and those regulating vocational training and related applied courses.

Capacity For Training

A massive expansion of training capacity is required if all the entrants to labour force are to acquire some vocational skills. New methods to enable skill building have to be created. More resources are needed and this requires new means to mobilise resources. The informal sector must receive special attention since it absorbs a large part of the labour force and enables the bulk of the new entrants to labour force to acquire working skills.

Skill Building and the Informal Sector

Training activity for entrants to organised sector has always received a highly preferential treatment in contrast to those working in the unorganised sector. This trend has only got accentuated in the recent phase of economic reforms. This is reflected in the exorbitant capitation fees for medical educationand the high fees in private establishments for newly emerging areas of employment like information technology -(IT) and IT-enabled services, engineering, hotel and catering, etc.

The problem had already got compounded even before reforms, because the formal training certificates became a screening mechanism for recruitment to the public sector/Government. Within the human resource development activity, literacy and general education always received greater attention from Central and State Governments than vocational training. In short, a policy is needed for skill building for the bulk of the new entrants to labour force for employment in the unorganised and the informal sector.

A strategy for skill building in the informal sector will be framed in the Tenth Plan. The elements of this strategy are:

— Government to articulate a policy framework for support of informal sector training.

— Use all available methods to increase literacy standards and production skills of persons in the informal sector.

— Certification system to declare competency in vocational skills acquired at work.

— Detailed surveys on training needs and existing arrangements for training in informal sector.

— Motivate associations in the informal sector to help develop skills and entrepreneurship.

— International agencies (such as the International Labour Organisation (ILO), United Nations International Children's Emergency Fund (UNICEF) and World Bank) to act in collaboration with the

Government at grass root level for administration and distribution of aid to informal sector.

— Opening training-cum-production centres in informal sector to enable individuals to earn while they learn e.g., handicrafts sector.

— Common identity cards by local bodies and police to those working in the informal sector clearly specifying the places where informal sector activity is not wanted.

— Refinancing for urban micro-credit that creates training facilities for this sector to open up entrepreneurship in this area.

— Private sector companies to be enabled to create foundations to finance communitybased programmes which include training and business support to micro-enterprises, coupled with tax and credit incentives.

— Identify organisations through which action programmes can be developed - tradebased guilds, trade unions and self-help groups.

— In the construction sector, the Building and Other Construction Workers Welfare Cess Act, 1996 enables generation of funds for the welfare of construction workers. A part of this can be utilised for financing the training of informal sector construction workers.

— Open Learning Systems for Vocational Skills.

Attracting Investment into Skill Building

Vocational skill building needs to be developed as an entrepreneurial activity in which the private sector would be willing to invest. Income tax incentives are available to higher technical and medical education establishments. These establishments can also draw resources from the market because of higher returns on such education.

Vocational skill building establishments need more income tax incentives than higher education establishments.

A skill development fund is envisaged to institutionalise the management, collection mechanism, contributions, and utilisation of funds. The resources collected should be utilised for creating training infrastructure in the area where they are collected. The purpose is to attract resources from the beneficiaries of training including the employers, the employees in the organised sector and the trade unions. Income tax incentives for these contributions could be considered.

Under Section 37(1) of the Income Tax Act, tax benefits for providing apprenticeship training is available to employers employing 500 or more workers. This benefit should be available to all establishments registered under the Factories Act, 1948, Shops and Commercial Establishments Act, (Central & State Acts), or any other relevant Act that enables setting up of institutions.

Equipment donated to vocational training institutes should be exempted from customs duties. In urban areas, schools and higher technical/professional/medical institutions get land at special rates. These institutions have a much higher income potential than the vocational training institutions, and, therefore, it is the latter that needs support and concessions in the allotment of plots and other civic infrastructure. This should be done especially in small and medium towns where the bulk of the new entrants to the labour force is located or can have easier access than the metropolitan towns.

Training By Governments at Centre and States

Much of the present capacity for training is provided by institutions financed by the Central and State

Governments. Most of the ITIs in the State sector, and the Central Government institutes are organised as subordinate offices of the respective governments. Examples of this are the establishments in sectors such as labour, technical education, health, small industry, agro and rural industries, and agriculture. In contrast, similar establishments under other departments like the Ministry of Information Technology are organised as autonomous bodies.

Administering these establishments through the normal governmental procedures greatly reduces the operational flexibility which a specialised institution needs. Such institutional structures also preclude the possibility of raising any resources from the trainees for financing at least a part of the cost. Thus, the discipline of a consumer-server relationship that accrues from claims against payments made is not easily possible in the existing departmental set up of the services rendered. These training and training related establishments should therefore be restructured as 'autonomous bodies'.

Autonomous bodies publish their accounts and a review of their performance and place them before the relevant legislature. This is more transparent than the operation of an attached office of government whose details of operations and accounts get absorbed in the voluminous accounts of the main ministry/ department. Under the departmental mode, all the revenue expenditure for salaries, raw materials, and maintenance of equipment is financed by the government budget directly to the training establishment. Sometimes, even the expenses related to travel and daily allowances are funded by Government through the training establishment.

Thus the department that owns the establishment finances not only the production of the training services but also the consumption of services produced by it. There is little or no exchange of services taking place and the trainees are faced with a 'take it or leave it' situation. While vocational training definitely serves a social purpose, the trainees should be allowed a choice of institutes.

Therefore, rather than funding the revenue expenditure to the institute, the trainees can be provided stipends through the local bodies, and they can choose among the approved institutes, which can either be Government establishments, Government-funded autonomous bodies, Government-aided institutes or private establishments. The performance of a training establishment will be reflected in the number of trainees attending it.

As a first step in the restructuring of ITIs, Central assistance for developing 100 State-run ITIs as institutes of excellence during the Tenth Plan will be extended to ITIs that are registered as an autonomous bodyand have a formal tie up with industry. In addition, financial aid given by State Governments to local bodies to introduce schemes for payment of stipend to vocational trainees for attending approved institutes will also be looked into. This will not have a burdensome impact on the budget because the funds given directly to training institutes for revenue expenditure will be reduced by a corresponding amount.

Policies and Programmes

The present system of governance of vocational training is nearly four decades old. The policy is framed at national level and the establishments that implement the policy are mainly at the state level. A national forum is useful for laying down guidelines but the transaction of business (for example, design of curriculum, recognition of institutes, conduct of examinations, award of certificates, etc.) has to be delegated to the field level or to autonomous professional bodies.

The National Vocational Training System (NVTS) is incontrast to education sector where the administrative responsibility is delegated to the State Governments and State Governments are in the process of delegating the responsibility for the administration of junior schools to panchayats and local bodies.. In the vocational training field, however, only a few states have 'State Councils for Vocational Training' that are active and there are no state-level organisations in fields of training not covered by the NVTS. Hence, most State Governments rely on the Central Government for operational decisions concerning their vocational training institutes.

In matters pertaining to vocational training, even the state-level arrangement cannot be sensitive to local needs. This is because vocational training has enormous linkages. It is concerned with the local employing establishments, the services needed by the local households, magnitude of new entrants to local labour force, the traditional skills available with local population, out-turn from local schools at Class VIII and Class X level, and the expectations of the local youth. Such interdisciplinary linkages can be established better at the district or block level, rather than at the national level.

Besides the Labour Sector of Plan, vocational training facilities exist in many other sectors. Most of these are national level efforts, and individually they are able to reach a very small part of the new entrants to the labour force. Each authority in charge of subject sets up training establishments in its field of specialisation. The target audience at the local level is the same set of households. The attempt to meet training needs through multiple authorities - labour, handlooms, handicrafts, small industry, education, health, women & child development, social welfare, tourism, etc. - does lead to redundancy at some locations. The local-level small industry establishments in the unorganised and the informal sector, and the local labour force do not derive benefits commensurate with the expenditure incurred by the Government.

Sometimes, the locations where the labour force has a high density of tiny establishments may not get reasonable attention from any of the training institutions set up by the Government. While each of the training initiatives has a definite area of specialisation, there is need for coordination amongst these and with the vocational training system at the district level, because the target beneficiaries are the same.

Information on the occupation profile of the labour force, wages, gap between skills required and available, the available and needed training facilities at district or block level is needed for framing training programmes sensitive to local needs. The nature of policy support required from the Government varies with the social and economic conditions in a district or block.

This covers liaison with industry, role of local industry/market/trade/self employed persons associations in guiding training and providing employment to trainees; role of associations/unions of workers; involvement or otherwise of NGOs; direct financial support to trainees versus incentives to the training establishment; institute-based versus industrybased apprenticeship training; provision of capital equipment or technology to training establishments; restructuring of existing institutes versus establishment of new institutes; inter-sectoral linkage among the developmental wings of governments; nature of interface with local education and labour administration; and relative roles for panchayat/district administration/local government/State Governments/ Central Government at a location.

In the Tenth Plan a district-level vocational training system will be evolved. A special group will be set up to suggest the modalities of designing and implementing a district-based vocational training system.

Training Of Youth in Rural Areas

With the diversification of agriculture and fresh opportunities in the rural non-farm sector, a number of new possibilities are emerging for employment in rural areas with better income. Besides the State Governments rural ITIs, the lead agencies of the Central Government are the Council for the Advancement for People's Action and Rural Technology (CAPART), Khadi and Village Industries Commission (KVIC), and the Community Polytechnics under the Ministry of Human Resource Development. The envisaged district-level vocational training system will be useful in developing programmes relevant for local rural needs.

The programme run by KVIC and CAPART impart skills as a part of the effort at establishing new production units and projects. Entrepreneurship development, besides training in production skills, is a part of the programme of these two organisations. These will be strengthened further in the Tenth Plan.

Training of Women

Certain occupations are preferred more by women. Training in such trades is included under the NVTS. State Governments have set up special women wings in ITIs and the Central Government has set up Regional

Vocational Training Institutes for women. Handlooms, handicrafts, and weaver development programmes provide training opportunities for women, along with the men. The women and child development sector includes development of self-help groups of women and training programmes.

There are special needs for vocational training for women, given the low female participation in the labour force, greater proportion of women in jobs which are of a seasonal or shortterm nature and the phenomenon of women resuming work after mid career breaks in the organised sector. Since setting up two parallel streams of training institutes for women and men will be too expensive, vocational training of women in existing institutes can be directly supported by paying stipends to women candidates and by supporting capital expenditure by institutes for specific trades. The women component of the Plan will also be used for getting a better share for women in the sector wise training initiatives.

Regions Requiring Particular Attention

The incidence of unemployment among the educated is higher in the northeast and in Jammu and Kashmir. The economic activities in these two regions are different from those in other parts of the country. A centrally sponsored scheme for doubling the capacity of ITIs in the northeast is being implemented. A similar scheme for Jammu and Kashmir is also envisaged.

Occupational Safety and Heath of Workers

Ensuring a reasonable quality of employment requires safeguarding of workers against risk and the occupational hazards. In a situation of labour surplus, the workers take up whatever work is available and are often exposed to risks. There are a plethora of laws that seek to safeguard the safety and health of workers. However, in practice, it is very difficult to enforce their compliance. The result is that the bulk of the workforce does not get a reasonable level of protection. Such tendencies get accentuated when market forces motivate the minimisation of the cost of labour input. Compliance with safety measures is confined to units in the organised sector.

Central Government establishments dealing with occupational safety and health provide mainly advisory and training services, except in the case of mines and ports and docks where enforcement is also with Central Government establishments like the Director General of Mines Safety (DGMS) and the Director General Factory Advisory Services and Labour Institutes (DGFASLI). Outside the labour sector, National Safety Council (NSC), located at Mumbai, sponsored by insurance companies and operating as a self-financing autonomous institution, conducts educational, training, promotional and consultancy services.

Typical industries, which are not covered by effective safety measures commensurate with the degree of exposure to risk, are:

- Agricultural workers
- Small mines
- Truck/buses operators
- Hotels
- Eating places
- Machinery repair establishments
- Beedi & cigar making
- tiny/small units
- Building construction

- Brick kilns
- Carpet manufacturing
- Fire works
- Power looms
- Home-based workers

To reach a majority of the workers, the focus has to be on the agriculture sector and on small establishments.

Agricultural Operations

There is a higher risk in agricultural occupations but it is difficult to administer safety regulations in this sector. Hence voluntary safety campaigns through agricultural universities and state agriculture departments are needed. Awareness campaigns to demonstrate the degree of risk and educate people about preventive measures should be conducted on television and radio. The Dangerous Machines Act, 1983, should be supplemented by positive efforts. Designs of agricultural equipment that are safe and those that are risk-prone should be displayed in the safety awareness campaigns.

Small Establishments

Clusters of small establishments have to be reached. Increase in worker productivity, reduction in worker fatigue, and curbing of disease needs to be established through safety audits and areas with a high density of poor workers and where work is done under extremely trying physical conditions should be selected for this. A recent study by International Labour Organisation (ILO) (2000-01) at Moradabad in Uttar Pradesh showed that only small investments in brass foundry chimney yielded substantial benefits. Improvements in designs of equipment were made after a study by technical consultants. To create a demonstration effect, such initiatives will be supported through the Plan. Awareness campaigns to disseminate success stories will also be supported.

The involvement of the insurance industry in promoting safety of workers in small establishments should be encouraged. Group insurance to share the risks of establishment owners should be promoted by the labour administration. A simple safety code for small establishments - whether factories, shops, establishments, building construction sites, road transport etc. - should be devised. This can be followed by umbrella legislation on occupational safety and health.

Safety as a profession should be developed on the same lines as accounting practice, cost accounting, company law compliance, asset valuation, insurance risk assessors, loss surveyors, etc. Establishments should be encouraged to have safety audit carried out. The practice of selfcertification based on adequate expertise should be encouraged. The NSC should establish its branches at the district level.

Review of Labour Laws

The employer-employee relationship cannot be left to be determined entirely in the market place based on a voluntary contract between the employer and employee because workers are not commodities and individual workers are the weaker party in any employeremployee relationship. Hence, legislations aimed at protecting the rights of labour are needed in a number of areas, e.g., to form unions for the purpose of collective bargaining, laying down minimum obligations which employers must meet with regard to social benefits, health and safety of workers, provision of special facilities for women workers, establishing grievance redressal mechanisms, etc.

The primary purpose of labour laws is to foster the growth of the employer-employee acknowledged relationship, in lieu of relationships based on voluntary contracts. Thus labour laws should enable the creation of jobs based on this acknowledged relationship. In the new economic scenario, the need for changes in labour laws has been emphasised. A fresh look at the structure of labour laws is, therefore, envisaged in the Tenth Plan. However, this task is to be seen in the perspective of the structure of the labour market. Labour laws are relevant for the wage employed, and not the self-employed. Out of the total estimated number of workers, 47.1 per cent are wage employed (Table 3) Among these, 25.3 per cent are in the agriculture sector where labour laws do not generally apply, 11.3 per cent are in the services sector and 10.2 per cent in manufacturing, mining and electricity, gas & water supply.

A good part of services is the employment in government establishments where the industrial labour laws do not apply. Among the wage employed, the labour laws apply to those hired on a regular salaried basis. Only about onethird of the wage employed are hired on a regular salaried basis. Of the 83 million workers covered by the Economic Census, 51.9 per cent are hired workers (Table 4)

Table 3. Structure of employment by industry and category of employment

Per cent

	Self Employed	Wage Employed	All Workers
Agriculture	34.5	25.3	59.8
Non-Agriculture :			
Manufacturing,	7.3	10.2	17.5

mining, electricity etc.			
Services sectors	11.1	11.7	22.9
All Activities	52.9	47.1	100.0

Table 4. Share of hired workers in all workers in enterprises covered by the Economic Census

Workers employed in	Agricultural enterprises	Non agricultural enterprises	All enterprises
Enterprises not hiring any worker	6.4	32.3	38.7
Establishments hiring workers	1.7	59.6	61.3
(share of hired workers in establishments)	(1.1)	(50.9)	(51.9)
All workers	8.1	91.9	100.0
Number of Workers (million)			83.30a

Thus the present structure of the labour market is such that the labour laws apply to a small part of the labour force. Hence, any immediate impact of changes in labour laws will be rather small. At the same time, the long-term objective is to increase the number of jobs, and, therefore, the goal is to substantially increase the present small share of employment that is based on some simple form of employer-employee contract.

The Government has already announced its intention to review some of the labour laws. Subsequently the Report of Second National Commission on Labour has suggested restructuring of labour laws. The Report is being examined by the Government. The restructuring of labour laws must bear in mind that small establishments employing less than 20 persons account for more than 60 per cent employment.

Small Establishments and Labour Laws

Labour laws are drafted uniformly for all enterprises and some exemption is provided under the common laws for smaller establishments. There is need to draft one single labour legislation applicable to all establishments employing less than 20 persons. Such legislation will provide for safety and social security of workers. Business linkages between large and small enterprises should be fostered and be utilised voluntarily by the large enterprise to deliver social security benefits to labour in the small enterprises

One of the reasons for rigidity in labour laws is that the 'employer' is expected to provide, individually, for security of employment (i.e., guarding against risks of loss of job, family sickness), retirement benefits and bear the costs of accidents and other occupation-related risk compensation. This happens because the labour market institutions, which are designed to provide social security to the workers, have a narrow reach, are almost exclusively administered by the Central Government, provide security at a high cost, are highly specific to individual employers and lack the concepts of 'shared risk'. Therefore, a more innovative and broad-based social security system for workers is needed to smoothen the process of labour reforms and enable rationalisation of labour laws.

Need For Making Changes in Certain Laws

The changes proposed in the Industrial Disputes Act, 1947 are meant to provide more flexibility in the hiring and firing of labour in order to increase productivity, efficiency and allow a more flexible adjustment process in the changing demand market. These proposals are being examined by the Government.

The repeal of the Contract Labour Act, 1947 will help provide more flexibility in recruiting labour without putting a long-term financial commitment on the employer. This, in turn, will encourage more recruitment. However, care should be taken to ensure that, in this process, more casualisation of labour does not take place. Already, the growth of casual labour in the 1990s is very high. A proper social security measure and a regulatory body to oversee the function of the recruiting agencies should accompany any change in the Act to safeguard the minimum quality of the job provided.

Placement agencies, which are utilised for hiring contract labour, should be registered. A forum to monitor placement agencies against exploitation of labour should be established. The principal employer should deliver unemployment benefits and pension to contract labour through placement agencies. The small-scale industry (SSI) sector plays an important role in economic development and contributes significantly to industrial output, employment, and export. However, the sector is burdened with maintenance of an unmanageable number of forms and registers under different labour laws.

The approach during the Tenth Plan would be to exempt it from the rigour of the various labour laws and make it vibrant and efficient. Efforts will, therefore, be made to conduct proper orientation and training programmes for the officers of the labour law enforcement machinery and create a positive climate for growth in this sector. The enforcement of various labour laws pertaining to SSI units falls under the jurisdiction of the State Governments. The entire onus of compliance in furnishing the returns and inspections falls on the entrepreneur. Most entrepreneurs cannot afford to engage a person exclusively for this purpose.

Therefore, the present system may be replaced by a system of self-certification wherein the return submitted on various labour laws by SSI units may be treated as prima facie compliance. Alternatively, a system of random inspection of a certain percentage of units on annual basis with well-defined criteria may be introduced.

The fact that labour laws are in the Concurrent List and are being implemented both by the Centre and the State Governments creates more complications. Various State Governments are demanding authorisation to carry out amendments in labour laws according to specific requirements. Since the State Governments are in the best position to enforce labour laws, in keeping with the prevailing socio-economic conditions in their states, the approach in the Tenth Plan would be to authorise them to amend labour laws as per their requirements.

In view of the increasing number of industrial disputes, industrial tribunals or labour courts are overburdened, affecting the speedy resolution of these disputes. Therefore, the approach in the Tenth Plan would be to set up Lok Adalats wherever necessary. In addition, the concept of social dialogue would be introduced where all concerned parties can participate to work out an amicable solution to major problems/issues in labour market reforms.

Framework Of Procedures, Administration And Related Services Concerning Labour Regulations

- As labour laws are in the Concurrent List, the State Governments may be permitted to make amendments as per their requirement.
- While carrying out amendments, the need for an adequate social safety net for the workers may be kept in mind.
- Formulation of schemes for pension and unemployment benefit for the unorganised sector

workers may be considered, depending upon the availability of resources.

— To avoid disproportionate regulatory burden on small-scale units, the present system of maintenance of various forms and registers under different labour laws may be replaced by a system of selfcertification and treated as prima-facie compliance.

— Inspection under the labour laws in SSI units may be conducted only on the basis of complaints by affected persons like workers, neighbours etc., or when absolutely essential in the interest of safety of workers in industry.

— Routine and periodic inspections of information technology establishments may not be necessary.

— Special quasi-judicial tribunals manned by officers of the labour department may take up hearing of disputes in case conciliation talks fails.

— Health, safety and welfare of the workers may be given due importance while reviewing the labour laws.

Social Security of Workers

Out of about 400 million workers in the country, only around 50 to 60 million are covered by some form of social security. For the rest, a job is the best guarantee for social security right now. However, the labour market is moving in a direction that change-over of jobs by an individual will become more frequent, public sector which provides a comprehensive social security cover to its employees, is shrinking in size, the pension system for government employees is under review, and more workers are seeking work in rural and urban informal sector, as the ability of agriculture to absorb workers diminishes.

Since any social security system stabilises over a period of 20 to 30 years, the efforts to be made in the Tenth Plan should have a long-term perspective. A budget-funded social security system similar to that available in developed countries is not feasible for India at present. Even in the present small base of coverage, a number of models to raise resources for social security are in use. Alternative models presently used for funding of Social Security of workers:

— Central Budget Funded – Plan

— Central Budget Funded– Non Plan

— State Budget Funded – Non Plan

— State Budget – Non Plan

— State Government Sponsored Insurance (Employer & Employee)

— Commodity Cess funded Welfare Funds

— Insurance Schemes

— Workers' Funded

— Self financed pension schemes

The annual resource flows in respect of a few selected schemes is of the order of Rs. 29,000 crore (Table 5). A more comprehensive listing of schemes will increase this. Thus, the economy is able to generate a sizeable volume of funds for social security even at present, though it may be small compared to the number of workers. Secondly, these funds are mobilised under some structured arrangements, which are specific to the category of workers covered. Therefore,new sources will have to be explored to cover additional category of workers.

Table 5. Resource flows In economy for social security – selected schemes

Scheme/ Institution	Rs. Crore/ year

1.	EPFO	10,700
2.	ESIC	1,500
3.	EPFO Pension Scheme	600
4.	LIC – Jeevan Suraksha	600
5.	Cess-based Central Welfare Funds	100
6.	State Government Welfare Funds	100
7.	SGRY	10,000
8.	NSAP	600
9.	Agricultural Workers- Central scheme	20
10.	Handloom Weavers – Thrift, Health & Group Insurance Schemes	5
11.	Central Government Employees Pension	4,000
12.	State Government t Employees Pension	NA
	Total (1-12)	29,125

The social security presently in use can be grouped under two categories organised sector and the unorganised sector. Though the organised sector social security systemcaters to a very small part of labour force, it has certain inefficiencies and weaknesses that need to be removed. A legislative and administrative framework has to be created for significant coverage of the unorganised sector by social security cover. The strategy would be to motivate and encourage the State Governments to formulate and implement schemes and programmes targeted at certain occupational groups in the unorganised sector without putting any additional pressure on the budget.

To extend the coverage of social security measures for the unorganised sector workers, setting up of the cooperatives, self-help groups, mutual benefit associations managed and financed by the occupational groups/workers and voluntary health insurance and pension schemes would be encouraged. Also, attention would be focussed on alternative income generating activities with the provision of credit arrangement for the supply of raw materials, etc. Awareness generation campaigns and dissemination of information to unorganised workers would be strengthened.

To improve the efficiency of the delivery mechanism of existing programmes for workers in the unorganised sector, local institutions like panchayati raj institutions (PRIs) and urban local bodies would be involved in monitoring the social security programmes. Considering the size of the country's workforce, a policy framework, at the national level, on social security provisions for different groups of workers and employees will be formulated. The following approach will be pursued:

Minimum Wages

— The Minimum Wages Act, 1948 may be amended enhancing the penalty for violations.

— A national policy on minimum wages may be evolved to help deal with the problem of inter-state variations in minimum wages. Presently, there are significant variations even in wages for the same occupations.

— The enforcement machinery for minimum wages in the Central and the State Governments may be strengthened with involvement of NGOs, and PRIs.

— To prevent exploitation of workers in the unorganised sector, awareness generation may be stepped up in collaboration with voluntary organisations, trade unions and other committed individuals. The Central Board for Workers Education can be entrusted with the task of awareness generation.

A Role For EPFO And ESIC

— The delivery of services in social security through the

Employees Provident Fund Organisation (EPFO) and the Employees State Insurance Scheme (ESIS) may be improved with the help of IT.

— Priority attention may be given to those social security covers for the unorganised sector, which can provide medical care, accident benefits, old age pension and maternity benefit.

— Provident fund schemes and Employees State Insurance schemes may be extended to the workers in the unorganised sector through innovative approaches. Innovative schemes may be launched on experimental basis targeting groups like rickshaw puller, auto rickshaw driver, head loader, etc.

Convergence Among Multiple Worker Welfare Schemes

— Emphasis may be given to the convergence of services for various social security measures undertaken by different ministries/departments.

— Community-based and location-specific social security measures may be encouraged through self-help groups, voluntary organisations, PRIs etc.

Central Funds for Welfare of Workers

— Based on the experience of the existing welfare funds for beedi, mine and cine industry workers, efforts may be made to constitute similar welfare funds for fish processing, salt workers, etc.

State Level Worker Welfare Funds

— State Governments may be encouraged to formulate and implement social security schemes for the unorganised sector as per their requirements with minimum burden on their budget.

— Concerted efforts may be made to enhance the coverage under the National Social Assistance Programmes (NSAP) for providing old age pension, maternity and other benefits to workers in the unorganised sector.

While an outline of possible initiatives is given here, a special group will prepare a perspective plan for social security for all workers. It would study the effectiveness of alternative models of providing social security to workers. The special group will examine the problems faced by other countries in implementing social security systems and their solutions.

Pension System for Unorganised Sector

The present pension system is confined to organised sector, which covers less than a tenth of the labour force employed. And even in the organised sector, there is no mechanism to generate earmarked resources for pension payments. Employers, who are mainly government and public sector, have severe financial limitations. And the organised sector pension systems, including those for the private corporate sector establishments, are designed for a single life-long employer-employee relationship. These features curtail the possibility of any significant expansion of coverage of workers by the pension system.

In the unorganised sector, there are a large number of self-employed persons with a reasonable level of income, but do not have a mechanism for earning a risk-free and reasonable return on their savings for retirement. And the low-income groups have no credible institution, where they can save during their active working life and earn an assured return for income support during retirement. Moreover, there is no prospect of a single employeremployee relationship in the unorganised sector, whether for the self-employed or for the wage employed.

The self-employed persons and the lowincome wage employed frequently take recourse to informal market, where the failure rate is high. In keeping with the announcement in the Union Budget 2001, Insurance Regulatory & Development Authority (IRDA) is preparing a road map for a pension system for the unorganised sector so that a self-sustaining pension system for unorganised sector can be introduced.

Vulnerable Groups In Labour Force

The groups that need particular attention are child labourers, bonded labourers, migrant labour, building and construction Workers and landless agricultural workers.

Child Labour

The best solution to this problem is compulsory primary education for all children. However, till this is achieved, special measures to curb child labour will include:

- Regular surveys to assess the number working children, and placing them in special schools.
- Imparting vocational skills to all children before they attain the age of 14 in schools set up under the National Child Labour Project.

Bonded Labour

The centrally sponsored scheme on the release and rehabilitation of bonded labour will continue. A new element of the scheme is the survey of bonded labour-prone locations. The effectiveness of the Bonded Labour Act 1976 primarily depends upon the identification of bonded labourers. Except specifying the functions of the vigilance committee, there is no inherent provision in the Act to force identification of bonded labourer. Therefore, the institutional mechanism in the shape of a vigilance committee would improve considerably if these bodies were broad based. Accordingly, it would be appropriate to induct some volunteers, including representatives from trade union organisations and local NGOs, as co-opted members in these committees. All vigilance committees should be reconstituted once in two years to ensure their proper functioning.

Migrant Labour

The Inter-state Migrant Workmen (Regulation of Employment and Conditions of Service) Act, 1979 There is a legislation to regulate inter-state flows of migrant workers through the contractors. Key actions are required both at the destination as well as at the point of origin of migration in order to reduce vulnerability and increase the capacities of the targeted social groups. Effective action requires the creation of a reliable information system for labour migration, as macro level data is often inadequate to capture the flow and pattern of migration.

Apart from estimating the magnitude of migration, the database may cover vital aspects like: causes of migration; processes of recruitment; occupational profile of migrants; working and living conditions of migrant workers; skill profile of migrants; expenditure and remittance patterns of migrant workers; status of enforcement of legislations like the Minimum Wages Act, 1948 Equal Remuneration Act 1976 etc. Initially such a survey may be undertaken in the major lending and borrowing districts and, thereafter, in other districts during the Tenth Plan.

Building And Construction Workers

Only four states have set up welfare boards provided under the Building and Construction Workers Welfare Cess Act, 1996. These welfare boards are meant to implement schemes like immediate assistance to beneficiary in case of accident, pension at the age of 60 years, premiums for group insurance scheme for the beneficiary and medical expenses etc. In the absence of such an administrative mechanism provided under the Act, resources could not be collected from construction contractors.

Table 6. Implementation status of the Building and Other construction Workers Welfare Cess Act, 1996

Building & other Construction Workers Welfare Board constituted[1]	Rules framed[2]	Expert committee constituted [2]
Kerala	Madhya pradesh	Andhra pradesh
Assam	West Bengal	Maharashtra
		Gujrat
		Uttar Pradsh
		Pondicherry
		Punjab
		Rajasthan
		Jammu & Kashmir
		Delhi

a—As on 20.08.2001

1—Notification of the Welfare Board by a State Government enables implementation of schemes for providing various welfare benefits to workers.

2—Expert Committee drafts the Rules for conducting business under the Act, and approval of Rules by State Government enables the creation of the Welfare Board.

Implementation of the Act by the State Governments will be pursued in the Tenth Plan. If necessary, giving some incentive to State Governments that implement the Act may be considered. Landless Agricultural Workers The main effort of Plan is poverty alleviation through rural development programmes. There is a need to ensure the effective implementation of the Minimum Wages Act, upgrading of skills, creation of awareness and introduction of social security measures, without putting serious burden on the government budget.

In the absence of a consensus among states on the Bill for the welfare of agricultural workers, state-specific approaches will have to be worked out. Some State Governments have introduced group insurance schemes to protect the workers against accidents and provide insurance in the case of death. Pension and other family benefits are available only in isolated cases, as for example, in Kerala. The number of workers to be covered is so large that the Central Government cannot by itself assume responsibility independent of the states.

The resources available with the Mandi Boards need to be tapped for this purpose. Some district-specific models for the welfare of this category of workers through one-time assistance could be explored. The problems of landless agricultural workers merit consideration under the agriculture sector reforms that have been initiated in the Union budget 2002-03.

Path Ahead

Much of the agenda for social and economic planning gets automatically addressed if the labour households get opportunities for gainful employment; are able to get a reasonable return for labour; have access to some insurance against risk of accident, death and against short spells of loss of work. Mechanisms by which some savings can be pooled, during the active working career, for an old age pension are also required.

The pre-requisite for improving the lot of the labour is the availability of gainful employment to the entire labour force. Macro-economic policies leading to 8 per cent GDP growth and promotion of labour-intensive sectors should enable the creation of more jobs than the additions to labour force in the Tenth Plan leading to a substantial reduction in the incidence of unemployment by the end of the Plan period.

Labour policy (including the measures taken for skill development and social security) has, by and large, focused on the organised sector, which has a very small share in the total labour force and, in any case, provides a reasonable level of income for its average worker. The infrastructure for the labour market that is presently available benefits only about 8 to 10 per cent of the labour force employed. Labour policy and programme in the Tenth Plan will focus on bulk of the labour force by taking up initiatives for those workers who are outside the private corporate and the public sector, i.e., in the so-called unorganised sector.

It is possible to reach out to the entire labour force through the labour market institutions over a period of five to ten years. This requires innovations in the existing policies concerning the labour market, and initiatives in a number of sectors that relate indirectly to work opportunities for, and income of, labour. Since the essential condition for improving the lot of the workers is the availability of gainful employment, the labour policy has to interact closely with the economic policy that concerns growth of labour intensive sectors, such as:

— Agricultural crop production, storage and marketing.

— Agro forestry, medicinal plants, bamboo development.

— Wasteland development and minor irrigation.

— Animal husbandry, livestock, horticulture, fisheries.

— Rural non-farm activities (rural development).

— KVIC.

— Small industries, including the weavers, the urban informal sector.

— Construction.

— Urban infrastructure services.

— Road transport and road construction.

— Retail and distributive trade.

— IT and communication services.

— Education and vocational training services.

— Women and child development services.

At present, most of these economic activities are dominated by the informal sector and the small and medium enterprises. Economic infrastructure to support these has to be strengthened. Support from micro-credit institutions and the insurance industry has to be provided to meet the capital needs and to cover risk in such ventures. Since, the nature of the activities listed above is not uniform, the labour policy must also take note of these variations. To reach out to the entire labour force employed, many of the existing institutions, laws and programmes have to be restructured. These pertain to:

— Reform of the vocational training system.

— Occupational safety and health.

— Labour regulations.

— Social security of workers.

Reform of the vocational training system will include measures to increase the demand for vocational training by linking it with the requirements of prospective employers. Recognising the role of the informal sector both as a principal provider of jobs and as a provider of on-the-job training, the vocational training policy has to specify a role for the informal sector. Noting the variations across locations in regard to employment opportunities, occupations, skill requirement, magnitude of and social characteristics of entrants to labour force, and traditional skills available, a district-level system for vocational training has to be developed.

The present national-level policies and programmes should only lay down guidelines, leaving implementation to the district-level authorities. To attract private capital into vocational training, skill building has to be developed as an entrepreneurial activity at par with technical and professional education. To ensure that the average worker is covered by occupational safety and health measures, programmes will be taken up for clusters with a high density of establishments and poor workers. Special programmes for labour-intensive high-risk activities will be taken up. Safety and risk awareness media campaigns to reach out to the workers in agriculture, small mines and road transport sectors will be taken up.

Since the number of small establishments is very large, all of which cannot be supervised directly by labour administration, occupational safety and health will be developed as a profession. Such professionals will supplement the efforts of labour administration in promoting compliance with labour standards. A new and simple labour law designed for small establishments, with the main objective of providing occupational safety and social security for workers, will be taken up. Shared risk concepts (social insurance) for bearing the risks faced by small establishments workers will be developed further.

At present, there are a number of models to provide some form of social security cover to the unorganised sector workers. A few states have set up welfare boards for unorganised workers. The EPFO and ESIC are developing models to demonstrate the provision of social security cover to the informal sector workers at specific locations. A role for associations of workers, and of the self-employed in the provision of social security has to be explored. Given the large resource requirements, and the experience in raising some resources through cess and other levies, the approach will be to provide social security through budget neutral measures.

Provision of a comprehensive social security cover to all workers is a gigantic task and requires adequate preparation. A perspective plan to provide social security cover to workers in agriculture, small establishments and in the informal sector will be prepared. The Tenth Plan will strive to ensure that, over a period of five to ten years, the labour market institutions for productivity improvement, safety, health and social security of workers cover the bulk of the labour force through simplified procedures. The outlay under Central Plan for Ministry of Labour for the Tenth Plan is Rs. 1500 Crore.

4

Food and Nutrition Security

The importance of optimal nutrition for health and human development is well recognised. At the time of Independence the country faced two major nutritional problems. One was the threat of famine and the resultant acute starvation due to low agricultural production and the lack of an appropriate food distribution system. The other was chronic energy deficiency due to:

— low dietary intake because of poverty and low purchasing power;

— high prevalence of infection because of poor access to safe-drinking water, sanitation and health care;

— poor utilisation of available facilities due to low literacy and lack of awareness.

The major public health problems were chronic energy deficiency (CED), kwashiorkor, marasmus and micronutrient deficiencies such as goitre, beriberi, blindness due to Vitamin-A deficiency and anaemia. The country adopted multi-sectoral, multipronged strategy to combat these problems and to improve the nutritional status of the population. Article 47 of the Constitution of India states that "the State shall regard raising the level of nutrition and standard of living of its people and improvement in public health among its primary duties".

Successive Five-Year Plans laid down the policies and strategies for achieving these goals.

The Green Revolution ensured that the increase in food production stayed ahead of the increase in population. The country has moved from chronic shortages to an era of surplus and export in most food items. The country is self sufficient in food grain production and currently there is a buffer stock of over 60 million tonnes. Along with the steps to achieve adequate production, initiatives were taken to reach foodstuffs of the right quality and quantity to the right places and persons at the right time and at an affordable cost.

Over the years, there has been improvement in access to food through the PDS; the food for work programme has addressed the needs of the vulnerable out-of-work persons. The ICDS programme aimed at providing food supplementation for pre-school children, pregnant and lactating women, nearly covers all blocks in the country. The Mid-day-meal programme aimed at improving the dietary intake of primary school children and reduction in the school drop out rates has been operationalised. There has been substantial improvement in access to health care. National programmes for tackling anaemia, iodine deficiency disorders and Vitamin-A deficiency are being implemented.

As a result of all these interventions, there has been a substantial reduction in severe grades of under-nutrition in children and some improvement in the nutritional status of all the segments of population. Kwashiorkor, marasmus, pellagra, lathyrism, beriberi and blindness due to severe Vitamin-A deficiency have become rare. However, several challenges remain. To meet all the nutritional needs of the growing population, the country will have to produce an extra five million tonnes of food grains annually and increase the production of livestock, fish and horticultural products. This has to be achieved in the face of shrinking arable land and farm size, low productivity, growing regional disparities in productivity and depletion of the natural resource base.

Appropriate steps have to be taken to minimise the potential adverse consequences of globalisation on domestic production, employment and price stability of food commodities. In spite of huge buffer stocks, 8 per cent of Indians do not get two square meals a day and there are pockets where severe under-nutrition takes its toll even today. Every third child born is under weight. Low birth weight is associated not only with higher infant mortality but also long-term health consequences including increased risk of non-communicable diseases. In the last five decades, the mortality rate has come down by 50 percent and the fertility rate by 40 percent but the reduction in under nutrition is only 20 percent. Around half of the pre-school children suffer from under-nutrition.

Micronutrient deficiencies are widespread; more than half the women and children are anaemic; reduction in Vitamin-A deficiency and iodine deficiency disorders (IDD) is sub-optimal. Under-nutrition associated with HIV/AIDS will soon emerge as a public health problem. Alterations in lifestyles and dietary intake have led to the increasing prevalence of obesity and associated non-communicable diseases. The country will have to gear itself up to prevent and combat the dual burden of under-nutrition and overnutrition and associated health problems.

Initiatives in the Tenth Plan

During the Tenth Plan there will be focused and comprehensive interventions aimed at improving the nutritional and health status of the individuals. There will be a paradigm shift from:

— household food security and freedom from hunger to nutrition security for the family and the individual;

— untargeted food supplementation to screening of all the persons from vulnerable groups, identification of those with various grades of under-nutrition and appropriate management;

— lack of focused interventions on the prevention of over-nutrition to the promotion of appropriate lifestyles and dietary intakes for the prevention and management of over-nutrition and obesity.

Interventions will be Initiated to Achieve:

Adequate availability of foodstuffs by:

— ensuring production of cereals, pulses and seasonal vegetables to meet the nutritional needs;

— making them available throughout the year at affordable cost through reduction in post harvest losses and appropriate processing;

— more cost-effective and efficient targeting of the PDS to address macro and micronutrient deficiencies. This may include providing coarse grains, pulses and iodised/ double fortified salt to below poverty line (BPL) families through the targeted PDS (TPDS);

— improving people's purchasing power through appropriate programmes including food for work schemes.

Prevention of under-nutrition through nutrition education aimed at:

— ensuring appropriate infant feeding practices

(universal colostrum feeding, exclusive breast feeding up to six months, introduction of semisolids at six months);

— promoting appropriate intra-family distribution of food based on requirements;

— dietary diversification to meet the nutritional needs of the family

Operationalising universal screening of all pregnant women, infants, preschool and school children for under-nutrition. Operationalisation of nutrition interventions for the management of under-nutrition through:

— targeted food supplementation and health care for those with under-nutrition;

— effective monitoring of these individuals and their families;

— utilisation of the panchayati raj institutions (PRIs) for effective inter-sectoral coordination and convergence of services and improving community participation in planning and monitoring of the ongoing interventions.

Prevention, early detection and appropriate management of micronutrient deficiencies and associated health hazards through:

— nutrition education to promote dietary diversification to achieve a balanced intake of all micronutrients;

— universal access to iodised/double fortified salt;

— early detection of micronutrient deficiencies through screening of all children with severe under-nutrition, pregnant women and school children;

— timely treatment of micronutrient deficiencies.

Promotion of appropriate dietary intake and lifestyles for the prevention and management of obesity and diet-related chronic diseases Nutrition monitoring and surveillance to enable the country to track changes in the nutritional and health status of the population to ensure that:

— the existing opportunities for improving nutritional status are fully utilized; and
— emerging problems are identified early and corrected expeditiously.

Research efforts will be directed towards:

— review of the recommended dietary intake of Indians;
— building up of epidemiological data on:
  — relationship between birth weight, survival, growth and development in childhood and adolescence;
  — body mass index norms of Indians and health consequences of deviation from these norms.

In view of the massive inter-state variations in the access to nutrition related services and nutritional status, state specific goals to be achieved by 2007 have been worked out taking the current status into account. National goals have been drawn taking into account the state specific goals.

Sustainable Food Production to Meet Nutritional Needs

One of the major achievements in the last 50 years has been the green revolution and selfsufficiency in food production. Food grain production has increased four-fold.

Interventions to Improve Food Production

Food grain production

Inputs needed to achieve a sustainable increase in food

grain production to meet the needs of the growing population have to be provided. Locally produced and procured coarse grains made available through the TPDS at a subsidised rate may substantially bring down the subsidy cost without any reduction in calories provided. This will also improve targeting as only the most needy are likely to buy these coarse grains. Millets are rich in minerals and micronutrients and hence increased consumption will improve the intake of these vital nutrients by the poor.

Pulse production

In the last two decades, there has been a progressive decline in pulse consumption, especially among the poorer segments of the population. This is due to stagnant production and the rising cost of pulses. This trend has to be reversed. Measures to improve pulse production may include reactivation of the pulse component of the Oil Seed and Pulse Mission, a major thrust on research and development and innovative community-based efforts similar to the M.S. Swaminathan Research Foundation's efforts in Tamil Nadu to improve pulse production.

Horticultural production

Available data on the current production of fruits and vegetables and the projected demand for 2006 are shown in Table 1. Per capita consumption of these in the country is very low. Consumption of adequate quantities of vegetables, especially green leafy ones, is essential for meeting the dietary requirement of vital micronutrients. Besides, vegetables also provide several phytochemicals and fibre.

At present, there is insufficient focus on the cultivation and marketing of low-cost, locallyacceptable green leafy vegetables, yellow vegetables and fruits. As a result, these vegetables are not available at affordable cost throughout the year. Health and nutrition education emphasising the importance of consuming these inexpensive but rich sources of micronutrients will not result in any change in food habits unless the horticultural resources in the country are harnessed and managed effectively to meet the growing needs of the people at an affordable cost.

Table 1. Fruits and vegetables (in million tons)

	Demand 2006	Production 1997/98
Fruit	50	40.05
Vegetables	130	72.83

Horticultural products provide higher yields per hectare and sell at higher prices. The processing, storage and transportation of horticultural products in a manner so that there is no glut and distress sales will make their production economically attractive to farmers and improve availability to the consumers.

Homestead production for dietary diversification

Homestead production is another method of increasing consumption of vegetables, milk and animal products and reduces the gap in consumption. Strategies can be worked out for using degraded lands for vegetable production.

Table 2. Per capita availability and deficit

Food Items	Per capita availability	ICMR dietary guidelines for Indians	Per capita deficit
Milk	216 g/day	300 ml/day	34 g/day

Egg	30 eggs/annum	180 eggs/annum	150 eggs/annum
Meat	3.24 kg/annum	10.95 kg/annum	7.71 kg/annum

Farm wastes as well as food grains unfit for human consumption can be used to feed backyard poultry in order to increase homestead production of eggs and chicken and also increase consumption of these at home.

Food Processing and Preservation

Post harvest losses especially in vegetables and fruits are presently in the range of 20 to 30 percent and contribute directly to higher costs and reduce availability of these commodities. Precision farming and food processing based on science and technology are both intellectually stimulating and economically rewarding, they can increase farmers' income and rural employment considerably. This will not only help in retaining educated youth in the farm sector but would also enable the micro-nutrient needs of the population to be met through a sustainable food-based approach.

Equitable Distribution of Foodstuffs

Achievement of food adequacy at the national level is a necessary, though not sufficient, precondition to ensure the achievement of household nutrition security. Buffer stocks do help to combat acute transient food scarcity, caused by natural disasters like floods and droughts. Early warning systems are in place and food can be rushed to areas of threatened distress fairly rapidly. What is proving more difficult is the task of combating chronic mild / moderate under-nutrition in a large number of poor households.

Inequitable distribution of available food among different segments of the population and even within the family is one of the major factors responsible for under-nutrition/over-nutrition. Good governance and health and nutrition education hold the key to improving equitable distribution of food based on need. The TPDS was introduced in June 1997 in an attempt to limit the mounting cost of subsidy, and at the same time, ensure that the BPL population does get subsidised food grains. Under this system subsidised foodgrains are provided only to people below the poverty line.

Taking the average household size as 5.51 (1991 Census), the monthly requirement of food grain for a household is 73 kg. TPDS meets only a part of the total requirement of food grains for the family. Apart from TPDS, other initiatives to improve food security of families include:

— allocation of food grains to institutions where indigent people live at rates similar to that for BPL population;

— Annapoorna Scheme (1998) to provide foodgrains to indigent old persons;

— Antyodaya Anna Yojana (2000) to provide food grains to the poorest of the poor families among the BPL population at the rate of Rs.2 per kg for wheat and Rs.3 per kg for rice;

— Sampoorna Grameen Rozgar Yojana (2001) for rural poor in need of wage employment; preference is given to scheduled castes, scheduled tribes and parents of children withdrawn from hazardous jobs.

Role of the Community

Innovative local efforts can go a long way in improving nutrition security especially for the poorer segments of the population living in vulnerable areas. Formation of local food grain banks under the supervision of the PRIs to help in achieving nutrition security for all and insulating the economically and socially deprived sections of the community from seasonal food insecurity has been suggested.

During the Tenth Plan period every effort will be made to:

— identify vulnerable groups/families, undernourished individuals and provide them with well-targeted subsidised food items through TPDS. In addition to the supply of rice and wheat, locally procured coarse grains, pulses and iodised salt may be provided;

— test and evaluate various modalities of improving the efficiency of the systems currently in operation to improve household nutrition security;

— choose appropriate modalities for making optimal use of available subsidies to meet the needs of the vulnerable segments of the population; and

— ensure that there is no duplication of schemes for improving nutrition security to vulnerable groups.

Transient Food Scarcity Due to Drought

Though the country has averted large-scale severe under-nutrition or famine in the past five decades, droughts do pose a major threat to food security. Over the years, the country has developed a system for the early recognition and management of transient food scarcity in times of drought. During the Ninth Plan period, Rajasthan, Andhra Pradesh and Gujarat were affected by drought. Of the various relief measures, Andhra Pradesh benefited only from additional ration through PDS. In the other two states, additional measures such as food for work, supply of drinking water, essential medicines and cattle feed were also in operation.

The National Institute of Nutrition (NIN), Hyderabad conducted a survey in the droughtaffected districts in these three states to assess the impact of drought and the ongoing intervention programmes on the diet and nutritional status of the population. In Rajasthan, there was no increase in prevalence of CED in adults (Body Mass Index <18.5) as compared to the non-drought period. However, there was an increase in the prevalence of under-nutrition in pre-school children (64.8 per cent) as compared to non-drought period (46.7 per cent). In Gujarat and Andhra Pradesh, prevalence of CED in children and adults was not more in the drought-affected districts. These data suggest that except in the case of children in Rajasthan, the adverse consequences of drought on the nutritional status were prevented due to intervention programmes.

During the Tenth Plan period, efforts will be made to monitor rainfall data to provide early warning of drought. Monitoring agricultural production will provide information about impending food insecurity. In drought-prone areas intensive monitoring of the nutritional status of pre-school children based on ICDS reporting system will help to assess the severity of the problem at block level. Timely relief measures can be organised based on these data. Apart from other process indicators for monitoring the relief operations, monitoring the nutritional status of pre-school children through the ICDS system will be used for assessing the out reach, adequacy and impact of relief measures.

Nutritional Status of Tribal Population

The tribal population is not a homogeneous group. There are wide variations among the groups in nutritional status and access to and utilisation of nutrition and health services. The tribal populations in the northeastern states have high literacy levels; they access available facilities, and hence their nutritional and health status is better than the national level. On the other hand, primitive tribes such as the Onges in the Andamans have very little awareness or access to either nutrition or health care.

Differential area-specific need assessment, strategies and programmes to improve access and utilisation of nutrition services have to be developed for each of the tribal areas. The tribal population is recognised as socially and economically vulnerable. Their lifestyles and food habits are different from that of their rural neighbours. They depend on minor forest produce, are employed in manual labour and may not have adequate income. Their food consumption pattern is dependent on the vagaries of nature and varies from extreme deprivation (in the lean seasons) to high intakes (in the post-harvest period).

Several focused interventions for tribal development and improvement in their health and nutritional status have been initiated in the last three decades. In order to assess the impact of these, the National Nutrition Monitoring Bureau (NNMB) carried out a repeat diet and nutrition surveys of the tribal populations living in the Integrated Tribal Development Project (ITDP) areas in 1998-99. These covered the states of Kerala, Tamil Nadu, Karnataka, Andhra Pradesh, Maharashtra, Gujarat, Orissa and West Bengal, where the NNMB had carried out an earlier survey in 1985-87.

Comparison of data of the two surveys showed that there has not been any improvement in the food and nutrient intake. However, there has been some reduction in the prevalence of severe forms of under-nutrition and in nutritional deficiency signs. The tribal population is more undernourished than their rural counterparts. There were substantial differences in the food and nutrient intake and nutritional status between tribal populations living in different states (Table 3). In some population groups, there was adequate intake of minerals and some micronutrients even though the diet was inadequate in terms of meeting energy and protein needs. The nutritional status of women and children in some of the northeastern states with a predominantly tribal population is better than the national average (Table 4).

Table 3. Inter-State Differences in Nutrient Intake

Nutrient Intake	State with Lowest	State with Highest
1-3 age-group		
Protein	10g	24.5g
Energy	466 k cal	1000 k cal
Vit. A	34 m g	264 m g
4-6 age-group		
Protein	19.8 g	36.3 g
Energy	756 k cal	1524 k cal
Vit. A	51.2 m g	502.7 m g
>18 years males		
Protein	47.0g	59.5g
Energy	1932k cal	2503k cal
Vit. A	82m g	575m g

Table 4. Nutritional Status in North Eastern States

State	% Tribal population as per 1991 Census	Weight-for-age (% below -3SD) in children < 3 years	% ever married women with Height below 145 cm	BMI < 18.5 kg/m²	BMI > 25 kg/m²
Arunachal Pradesh	63.7	7.8	11.9	10.7	5.1

Meghalaya	85.5	11.3	10.3	18.8	10.8
Mizoram	94.8	5.0	21.1	25.8	5.8
Nagaland	87.7	7.4	10.7	22.6	5.3
All-India	8.1	18.0	13.2	20.3	10.6

During the Tenth Plan, monitoring nutritional status of the tribal population, especially of those who have poor access to services, will be continued. Monitoring of the ICDS reporting will provide early warning of any deterioration in the nutritional status in pre-school children so that appropriate intervention can be initiated. Research studies on dietary habits that contribute to good nutritional status as well as those that make the tribal population vulnerable to diseases will be carried out. Based on the data, specific intervention programmes will be taken up to improve nutritional eand to eliminate dietary habits that are likely to cause ill health.

Energy Requirements of Indians

Energy requirement is defined as the amount that will balance the energy expenditure of the individual (as determined by body size and composition and level of physical activity) consistent with long-term good health. This intake will allow for the maintenance of economically necessary and socially desirable physical activity. In children and pregnant/ lactating women, the energy requirement will include energy needed for deposition of tissue and secretion of milk at the rate consistent with good health. All estimates of requirement are based on habitual intakes and though these are expressed as daily intake, it is not implied that these amounts must be consumed on a daily basis. Estimates of requirement are derived from actual data of individuals on intake and expenditure.

Actual intakes and expenditure of people of the same age, sex, similar body size and performing similar physical activity are used to compute average energy requirement for the groups. The recommended intake of energy of a group is equal to the average energy requirement of individuals of the group because both lower and higher energy intake are associated with health hazards. This is in contrast to other nutrients.

For example, the recommended safe level of protein intake is the mean +2 SD value of the group because with this over 97 per cent of the persons in the group would get their requirements. Studies have shown that Indians have about 5 per cent lower Basal Metabolic Rate (BMR) than those predicted on the basis of WHO/FAO/ UNU equations. The possible causes of lower BMR among Indian include:

— under-nutrition with low body weight and low BMI (weight in kg/ height in metre^2);

— under-nutrition resulting in lower protein turnover (which accounts for 20 per cent of BMR);

— difference in proportion of muscle and viscera;

— lower oxygen supply to the muscle;

However, the energy cost of work done computed in terms of basal energy cost or physical activity ratios are similar. For computing RDA, the ICMR has taken body weight of 'reference man' as 60 kg and that of 'woman' as 50 kg. Average weight of Indian men is 52 kg and women 44 Kg. For children and adolescents, weight for age from NCHS / well-todo Indian children have been utilised by ICMR for deriving the RDA so that energy intake enables optimum growth.

However, as in adults, majority of children and adolescents weigh substantially less and hence their energy requirement is lower. In view of these, it is likely that the energy requirement of Indians is likely to be substantially lower than the current ICMR recommendations (Table 5). Over the last few decades there has been a reduction in the physical activity and hence reduction in the energy needs in all the age and weight categories. Obesity rates in all age groups are increasing mainly because of the reduction in physical activity without concomitant reduction in energy intake.

Table 5. ICMR's RDA for Energy (reference body weights and actual body weights)

Sex	Ref.Body weight	Actual body weight	Energy RDA			
			Activity category	For Ref. Body Weight	For Actual body Weight	Percent difference
			Sedentary	2425	2115	13
Man	60.0	52.0	Moderate	2875	2492	13
			Heavy	3800	3293	13
			Sedentary	1875	1740	12
Woman	50.0	44.0	Moderate	2225	1958	12
			Heavy	2925	2594	11

In view of the known adverse health consequences of both excess and deficient energy intake, it is essential that appropriate recommendation for the RDA for Indians is evolved. This has to be done quickly as the country is entering an era of dual disease burden of CED and infections on the one hand and that of obesity and non-communicable diseases on the other.

During the Tenth Plan, review of the RDA for Indians will be taken up on a priority basis. The ICMR has reconstituted its Expert Committee on RDA which will take all the above factors into consideration and come up with an appropriate recommendation regarding the dietary intake of Indians. One of the priority areas of research during the Tenth Plan will be studies to define the BMR and energy requirement of healthy adult Indian men and women, adolescents, children and the elderly. Simultaneously studies will be taken up to define the dietary intake needed to correct the chronic energy deficiency or obesity in each of these groups.

Assessment of Nutritional Status

Anthropometric indices (height, weight and BMI) are widely used for the assessment of the adequacy of energy intake. Body weights and heights of children reflect their nutritional and growth status; weights and heights of adults represent the cumulative effect of dietary intake over a long period. The BMI is the most widely used anthropometric index for the assessment of the nutritional status in adults as it reflects the effect of both acute and chronic energy deficiency/excess. BMI, however, does not clearly bring out the entire extent of chronic under-nutrition.

For instance those who are stunted and have low body weight may have normal BMI. An increase in energy intake will result in improvement in BMI both in adults and in children, but in adults and children with severe stunting, improvement in dietary intake will not result in an improvement in height. Continued overconsumption of energy especially in stunted individuals could lead to over-nutrition, obesity and increased risk of non-communicable diseases. It has also been reported that the body fat content for a given BMI is different not only between men and women but also among countries (Table 6). BMI has been used to assess energy deficiency as well as energy excess.

The currently used norms (<18.5 - undernutrition and >25 overweight) were evolved on the basis of data from the developed countries where adverse health consequences of under-nutrition have been shown to be associated with BMI values below 18.5 and the health hazards of over-nutrition have been reported with BMI of over 25. The mean and frequency distribution of BMI of Indians are substantially different from developed countries. It is, therefore, possible that the currently used classification may be satisfactory for developed countries but not for India.

Table 6. Variability of body fat at BMI 20 among rural population of three countries

Country	% Body fat	Fat mass (kg)		Assuming fat
		Male	Female	= 0 then BMI
Papua New Guinea	1	1	6	19.7
Ethiopia	7	4	8	18.0
India	12	6	8	16.9

There are wide variations in height, weight, body composition and BMI right from birth through childhood and adolescence between countries and different income groups in the same country. Birth weight and growth of Indian children from wellto-do segments of the population are similar to United States National Center of Health Statistics (NCHS) standards but adult heights and weights in India are lower. The functional significance of inter-country variations in stature are not yet clearly understood.

However, the existing gap between the stature of Indians from well-to-do families where there are no nutritional constraints and under-nourished persons from poorer segments of the population is clearly due to poor nutrition and health care. The short-term nutritional goal of the country is to identify individuals and families, who are under-nourished and provide them with adequate nutrition and health care so that they do not incur health hazard associated with undernutrition.

As both CED and obesity are associated with adverse health consequences, it has been suggested that each country should develop its own norms for BMI and cut-off points indicative of various degrees of under-nutrition and over-nutrition based on their own data on health problems in persons with varying BMI levels. In view of the profound implications of these suggestions it is essential that research studies are taken up during the Tenth Plan period to examine the usefulness of currently used cut-off points of BMI as indicators of CED, metabolic functions, work capacity and health indices.

It is also important to collect data on BMI of well-nourished Indians in different regions and the health profile of adults with different BMI. Epidemiological data on the risk of noncommunicable diseases among different BMI groups in India will have to be collected to evolve appropriate cut-off points for BMI in Indians so that those at risk can be identified and appropriate interventions undertaken.

Dietary Intake and Nutritional Status of Adults

There have been substantial changes in the socio-economic status of people, some increase in the dietary intake of men and women especially of the affluent segments in rural and urban areas, ready availability of fast foods, ice creams and other energy rich food items at affordable costs have resulted in increased energy consumption. About 48 per cent of the households consumed more than adequate amount of both proteins and calories, while 20 per cent of households consumed inadequate amounts of both the nutrients.

With increasing access to cooking gas, piped water supply, labour-saving gadgets and transport, there has been a substantial reduction in the physical activity pattern and energy expenditure, especially in the middle and upper income groups. Data from NNMB repeat surveys indicate that there has been some reduction in under-nutrition and some increase in obesity over the last two decades. Data from National Family Health Survey-2 (NFHS) confirms that currently both under-nutrition and over-nutrition are problems in women (Table 7) and that there are massive inter-state differences.

Table 7. Nutritional Status of ever married women aged 15-49

	BMI < 18.5 (kg/m^2)	BMI > 25 (kg/m^2)
All India	35.8%	10.6%

The percentage of women with under- nutrition varies from 10.7 in Arunachal Pradesh to 48 in Orissa and those who are overweight from 3.7 in Bihar to 33.8 in Delhi. The country will, therefore, have to gear up to prevent, detect and tackle the problems of both under-nutrition and over-nutrition in the next two decades.

Over the last two decades there have been a growing number of reports that Indians are a very high-risk group for cardiovascular diseases and diabetes. A majority of them are not obese and do not have risk factors associated with non-communicable diseases in the developed countries. The higher prevalence of non-communicable diseases among persons whose birth weights were low has been documented. It has been hypothesised that people who have lived under nutritional constraints over millennia have 'thrifty genes' which enable them to survive and sustain themselves with lower energy intake.

In such a population, any rapid increase in energy intake may result in increased risk of non-communicable diseases. This is an area where further research studies need to be done. The amount by which the dietary intake should be increased or decreased to correct CED/ obesity in adults will depend upon the rate at which the desirable weight is to be achieved and the extent to which the deficit or excess in weight is due to lean and fat tissue. Since adults cannot grow, the appropriate weight for actual height is to be calculated and the appropriate dietary intake to correct under-nutrition or over-nutrition computed.

In adults who are seriously underweight for their height, there will generally be a loss of both fat stores and lean body mass. Therefore, bringing their weight into the normal range requires additional amounts of both energy and protein. Clinical experiences suggested that under-weight adults who are free from disease could be rehabilitated fairly rapidly if they eat to appetite. For correction of obesity, a low energy diet coupled with adequate exercise will be needed. If low energy diet is to be continued for a long period to achieve desired reduction in weight, it is essential to ensure adequate amounts of protein and micronutrients intake.

For sedentary adults food low in energy density, rich in fibre containing lot of vegetables and adequate exercise would go a long way in terms of providing satiety and preventing obesity. During the Tenth Plan, the major thrust would be to undertake massive health and nutrition education to encourage appropriate dietary intake and healthy life styles among all segments of the population. Epidemiological studies will be initiated to obtain data on dietary intake, nutritional and health status to define levels at which functional impairment in health status occur.

Geriatric Nutrition

With increasing longevity, the proportion and number of persons in the age group of 60 years and beyond is rapidly increasing, with women out- numbering men. The population of elderly has been projected to double from 6.23 crore in 1996 to 11.29 crore in 2016. With increasing age, there are metabolic changes and also reduction in physical activity and, as a result, their energy requirement is substantially lower than younger adults. Elderly individuals face problems in ensuring appropriate dietary intake because of alteration in taste with increasing age and loss of teeth.

The reduction in physical activity with increasing age, not accompanied by a concurrent reduction in energy intake, makes the elderly prone to obesity. Due to low intake of vegetables, food rich in micronutrients and increased susceptibility to infection, anaemia and Vitamin B complex deficiency may be more common in the elderly. Adequate dietary calcium intake from birth to 30 years is critical for the development of peak bone mass. Osteoporosis occurs more commonly in women than in men as bone loss occurs earlier and more rapidly in women as compared to men.

With increasing longevity, there will be an increase in the number of persons with osteoporosis. There is very little data on the incidence of osteoporosis in India. Lack of social support, breaking up of the joint family system, changing lifestyles all aggravate the health and nutritional problems of the elderly. Available data from nutrition surveys indicate that the dual problem of chronic energy and micronutrient deficiency on the one hand and obesity on the other are seen among the elderly. Innovative efforts to provide societal support, health care and nutrition services to the elderly are currently being taken up by several agencies.

Simultaneously, there are efforts to improve family and societal support to elderly within the existing cultural ethos in different regions. Successful models for improving quality of life will have to be replicated. In many states elderly persons who are without any financial support get old age pension. The amount as well as coverage varies between states but, on the whole, the amount provided is too low to meet the nutritional needs of the elderly person. Following reports of severe undernutrition among the elderly and destitute persons in several states, the central and the state governments initiated steps to improve the access of these segments to food-grains.

The National Policy on Older Persons announced in January 1999 provides a framework for welfare of the elderly persons including improved financial security and increased access to health and nutrition services. It is envisaged that National Plan of Action for the implementation of the policy will be drawn up. The policy also recommends research to expand the knowledge base on nutritional needs of the elderly. During the Tenth Plan, a database on the magnitude of the nutritional problems in the elderly will have to be created through the ongoing diet and nutrition surveys. Based on the data appropriate area- specific intervention programmes can be drawn up. While the technical inputs will come from the nutritionists, implementation of the programme will largely rest with the families, community and the PRIs.

Nutritional Status of Adolescents

Projections made by the Technical Group on Population Projections indicate that the number of adolescents will increase from 200 million in 1996 to 215.3 million in 2016. Adolescents, who are undergoing rapid growth and development, are one of the nutritionally vulnerable groups who have not received the attention they deserve. Adolescents gain 30 per cent of their adult weight and more than 20 per cent of their adult height between 10 and 19 years. Taking into account, the desirability of achieving full potential for growth, ICMR has used NCHS/well-to-do Indian children's body weight for computing RDA for adolescents.

However, children from the poorer segments of the population in India are shorter and weigh less. It is unlikely that any extra food at this stage can accelerate or extend the duration of physical growth. Additional dietary intake at this period can only lead to adolescent obesity. The ICMR Expert Committee for RDA may have to take all these into account and evolve appropriate recommendations for dietary intake in Indian adolescents. Data from the NNMB repeat surveys have shown that there has not been any substantial increase in the dietary intake of adolescents; but there has been some improvement in height (2.5-3.5 cms), weight (1-1.5 kg) and BMI between 1975-79 and 1995-97.

Data from NNMB also shows that over this period there has been some increase in obesity among adolescents especially for those from the affluent groups both in the urban and rural areas. The prevalence of micronutrient deficiencies are high. With the onset of menstruation, girls in this age group are vulnerable to anaemia and all its adverse consequences. Data from NFHS-2 indicate that the median age at marriage of girls in India is 16 years and 61 per cent of all girls were married before the age of 18. There are large inter-state variations in age at marriage.

The mean age at first birth is 19.2. Under-nutrition, anaemia and poor antenatal care inevitably lead not only to increased maternal morbidity but also to higher incidence of low birth weight and peri-natal mortality. Poor childrearing practices of these girls will add to infant morbidity and under-nutrition, thus perpetuating the intergenerational cycle of under nutrition. Appropriate education, nutrition and health interventions, delay in age at marriage, optimum health and nutrition interventions during pregnancy are some of the inter-sectoral initiatives to break this vicious cycle.

With a view to minimising these adverse effects, appropriate nutritional and health interventions for adolescents are being taken up under the ICDS and Reproductive and Child Health (RCH) Programmes. The Department of Women and Child Development has launched Kishori Shakti Yojana (2000). Prime Minister in his Independence day address in 2001 stated that food grains will be provided to combat under-nutrition in adolescent girls and pregnant and lactating women. A pilot project is being initiated to operationalise the announcement of the Prime Minister. The project, initially for a period of two years, will be taken up in two of the backward districts in each of the major states and most populous district (excluding the capital district) in the remaining smaller states/Union Territories.

The funds for 2002-03 is being given as special additional central assistance to the states so that they can provide food grains through TPDS totally free of cost to the families of identified under-nourished persons. The programme will be operationalised through the Department of Women and Child Development in the centre and in the states. During the Tenth Plan, studies to improve the understanding of the relationship between energy requirements, body composition, endocrine changes and micronutrient status in children and adolescents will be taken up so that appropriate focused interventions can be initiated. Programmes to improve the nutrition and health status of adolescents will be effectively implemented.

Adolescent girls fall into two categories — those who are in school and those who are not. The focus of efforts to improve the health and nutritional status of those who are in school will have to be through the school health system. Efforts will be made to screen all for anaemia and undernutrition and provide appropriate management. Screening will also enable the identification of obese adolescents and the initiation of appropriate remedial measures. Appropriate information, education, communication and motivation (IECM) to delay marriage until at least the age of 18 and postpone child-bearing till the age of 20 will be vigorously taken up.

A majority of the girls in the out-of-school category marry during their early teens and conceive soon after. The focus of any strategy will be to get these girls to the anganwadi so that the anganwadi worker, in collaboration with the auxiliary nurse midwife (ANM), can undertake the following activities:

— screening for under-/over-nutrition and micronutrient deficiencies;

— targeted interventions to tackle the nutritional problems of adolescents, especially girls;

— introduction of community-supported supplementary nutrition programmes using community food and food prepared by women's groups using locally-available commodities and given on a priority basis to adolescent girls who are under-nourished or pregnant;

— IEC to improve awareness;

— health and nutrition education to prevent early pregnancies and under-nutrition; and

— appropriate antenatal and intrapartum care and contraceptive care when needed

Nutritional Status of Pregnant and Lactating Women

Traditional belief was that pregnant and lactating women require additional dietary intake as they have to meet their own nutritional requirements and also supply nutrients to the foetus and the infants. Some available data indicated that a low dietary intake, especially in already chronically undernourished women, had adverse effects on the health and nutritional status of the mother, the course and outcome of pregnancy and the birth weight of the offspring. Both the ICMR and the WHO Expert Groups recommended additional intake for pregnant and lactating women.

The WHO had recommended an additional 300 kilo calories (Kcal) throughout pregnancy and 500 additional Kcal during the first year of lactation. The ICMR has recommended an additional intake of 300 Kcal during the second and third trimester of pregnancy, 550 Kcal during the first six months of lactation and 400 Kcal during 7- 12 months of lactation. Epidemiological data from the developed and developing countries, however, indicate that there is no increase in dietary intake during pregnancy and lactation among habitually wellnourished women who eat to appetite. This did not have any adverse effect either on their own nutritional status or on the course and outcome of pregnancy.

There is a reduction in BMR and physical activity and there might be some improvement in the as yet unmeasured efficiency of energy utilisation. The energy and nutrients saved due to these adaptive processes are sufficient to meet the increased requirements for nutrients during pregnancy. So long as there is no reduction in the habitual dietary intake, there is no deterioration in the maternal nutritional status either during pregnancy or during lactation.

In wellnourished individuals, additional intake during pregnancy and lactation results in excessive weight gain and this may lead to obesity. However, there are limits to adaptations. Studies from developing countries have shown that reduction in dietary intake below habitual levels and increased workload above the habitual levels are associated with deterioration in maternal nutritional status and reduction in birth weight. Some such readily identifiable situations are:

— reduction in habitual dietary intake during drought and the pre-harvest season;

— increase in work e.g., newly inducted manual laborers;

— combination of both the above (food for work programmes);

— adolescent pregnancy;

— pregnancy in a lactating woman; and

— pregnancy occurring within two years after last delivery.

Research studies in India and elsewhere have shown if pregnant women in whom there has been a reduction in habitual dietary intake or excess energy expenditure or whose body weight is less than 40 kg are identified and given adequate continuous food supplementation and antenatal care there is substantial improvement in outcome of pregnancy, birth weight and neonatal mortality. Encouraged by such data, almost all developing countries embarked on food supplementation programmes for pregnant and lactating women. None of these programmes screen pregnant women or provide supplements only to those with energy gap or those with moderate/severe undernutrition.

When food supplements are provided without screening, targeting supplementation and monitoring the programme, the improvement in maternal nutrition, and birth weight, if any, is very limited. One of the major problems is to reach food supplements to the undernourished women. Even when the logistics of reaching the food to women is meticulously worked out and efficiently carried out, food sharing patterns within the family results in the 'target' women not getting the supplements in significant quantities. Obviously this is one of the factors responsible for the demonstrated lack of beneficial effect. The lack of adequate antenatal care and continued physical work during pregnancy are two other factors responsible for the lack of impact.

Under the ICDS programme, food supplements are being provided to pregnant and lactating women who come to anganwadis. The reported coverage is between 15 and 20 per cent in most blocks. The women who receive supplements are not being chosen on the basis of their nutritional status and may not be the most needy ones. There has not been any evaluation studies on this component of the ICDS. However, data from nutrition surveys indicate that there has not been any significant decline in maternal undernutrition over the last decade.

During the Tenth Plan efforts will be made to weigh all women as early in pregnancy as possible and to monitor their weight gain. Wellnourished women will be advised not to increase their dietary intake to prevent over nutrition and obesity. Women who weigh less than 40 kg will be identified and

— given food supplements consistently throughout pregnancy;

— given adequate antenatal care;

— monitored for weight gain during pregnancy and, if weight gain is sub-optimal, identify the causes and attempt remedial measures; and

— given appropriate antenatal, intrapartum and postpartum care.

Effective intersectoral coordination between ANMs and anganwadi workers will enable the identification of and provision of appropriate care to undernourished pregnant women. The PRIs can play an important role by ensuring that these women receive food supplement throughout pregnancy. The methods by which food supplements can be provided to identified undernourished pregnant and lactating women may vary. In some cases the food may be provided at the work site. In yet other cases, it might be possible to link antenatal care and the provision of free foodgrains for pregnant and lactating women on lines similar to the Mid-day-meals scheme to increase enrolment.

With the empowerment of the PRIs and nagar palikas, it might be possible to monitor these programmes at the local level and consequently achieve better coverage. If welltargeted intervention to identify undernourished women and provide them health and nutrition education and ante-natal care are implemented effectively, there can be substantial reduction in severe under-nutrition in pregnant women and low birth weight. The feasibility, utilisation, cost and impact of such well-directed, innovative strategies involving close local monitoring need to be assessed.

Maternal Nutrition and Birth Weight

It is estimated that one-third of Indian neonates weigh less than 2.5 kg at birth. There are substantial differences in the maternal body weight and birth weight between income groups, which are partly due to differences in the nutritional status and partly due to differences in health care (Table 8).

Efforts to improve these through appropriate health and nutrition interventions are dealt with in the section under Family Welfare. A majority of deliveries occur at home. Identification of infants weighing less than 2.2 kg and referring them to hospitals where a paediatrician is available will substantially reduce neonatal mortality.

Table 8. Birth Weight and Socio-economic Status

	Poor Income	Middle Income	High Income
Age (years)	24.1	24.3	27.8
Parity	2.41	1.96	1.61
Height (cm)	151.5	154.2	156.3
Weight (kg)	45.7	49.9	56.2
Hb (g/dl)	10.9	11.1	12.4
Birh weight (kg)	2.70	2.90	3.13

During the Tenth Plan, efforts will be made to ensure that the anganwadi workers report all births in the village, weigh all neonates delivered at home soon after birth and refer those weighing less than 2.2 kg to a hospital with a pediatrician. This will enable development of referral services, reduce neonatal mortality and generate nation-wide data on birth weight and prevalence of low birth weight.

Growth During Infancy

Energy requirements during infancy are very high because this is one of the periods of very rapid growth. The energy cost of growth in infants and children include two components: the energy value for the tissue and the energy cost of synthesising the tissue. This has to be taken into account along with the basal energy needs and energy needs for activity in infants and children.

Available data suggest that energy needs are highest during the first three months and then fall over the next six months when the growth rates are lower. It rises again after nine months as the child becomes physically more active. The RDA for infants drawn up both by WHO and by ICMR takes this phenomenon into account (Tables 9 and 10).

Table 9. RDA of infants and children

	Energy (kcal)	weight (kg)
3-6 months	700	7
6-9 months	810	8.5
9-12 months	950	9.5

Table 10. RDA of infants and children

	Energy (kcal)	weight (kg)
<6 months	583	5.4
6-12 months	844	8.6

Growth during infancy and childhood depend upon birth weight, adequacy of infant feeding and absence of infection. Available data clearly indicate that in India exclusively breastfed infants thrive normally during the first six months of life and have lower morbidity episodes than those receiving supplements in addition to breast milk. In view of this, promotion of universal exclusive breast-feeding for the first six months of life has been the national policy. Breast milk alone is insufficient to meet the growing baby's needs after six months and appropriate semisolid complementary foods have to be introduced to enable them to meet their nutrient needs. Care should be taken to reduce the chances of infection by providing freshly prepared food.

In India, steps taken for the protection and promotion of the practice of breast-feeding have been effective and breast feeding is almost universal. However, the message that exclusive breast feeding up to six months and gradual introduction of semisolids after that are critical for the prevention of under-nutrition in infancy has not been as effectively communicated. Data from NFHS-2 indicated that exclusive breast-feeding among infants in the age group of 0-3 months was only 55.2 percent. In spite of the emphasis on the need for timely introduction of complementary food only 33.5 per cent of the infants in the age group of 6-9 months received breast milk and semi- solid food.

There are substantial inter-state differences in exclusive breast feeding and timely introduction of semi-solid food. While Andhra Pradesh and Kerala fare well in terms of appropriate infant feeding practices, the too early introduction of supplements is a major problem in states like Delhi, Himachal Pradesh and Punjab and too late introduction of supplements is a big problem in Bihar, Uttar Pradesh, Madhya Pradesh, Rajasthan, and Orissa. Both these practices are associated with increased risk of under-nutrition and infection. As a result of these faulty infant feeding habits, there is a steep increase in the prevalence of under-nutrition from 11.9 per cent at less than 6 months to 58.5 per cent in the 12- 23 months age group.

Correction of these faulty infant feeding practices through nutrition education will prevent the steep increase in under-nutrition in the 6-24 months age group. During the Tenth Plan the major focus will be on

— promotion of exclusive breast feeding in the first six months;

— nutrition education for the introduction of appropriate low-cost, energy dense complementary food at six months of age;

- three-monthly monitoring of weight in infancy and childhood; and
- detection of infants with faltering growth and initiating appropriate steps to improve their nutritional status.

Studies carried out at the NIN had shown that if roasted coarsely ground cereals, pulses and oil seeds mixture is provided to households free of cost, the mothers were willing and able to give this to young children three to four times a day; as a result there was improvement in timely introduction of complementary food. In an effort to find out if this could be replicated at the national level, Additional Central Assistance is being given since 2000-01 under the nutrition component of PMGY to provide such a mixture once a week to BPL families totally free of cost. The progress and impact of this will be assessed during the Tenth Plan period.

The goals for the Tenth Plan are to

- enhance early initiation of breast-feeding (colostrum feeding) from the current level of 15.8 per cent (as per NFHS 2) to 50 per cent;
- enhance the exclusive breast-feeding rate for children up to the age of six months from the current rate of 55.2 per cent (as per NFHS 2) to 80 per cent; and
- enhance the complementary feeding rate at six months from the current level of 33.5 percent (as per NFHS 2) to 75 per cent.

Health - Nutrition Interactions

Dietary intake is a critical, but not the sole, determinant of the nutritional status of the population. Low birth weight, poor infant feeding practices, infections due to poor sanitation, lack of safe drinking water and poor access to health care are other major factors responsible for undernutrition. In spite of low dietary intake, the prevalence of severe under-nutrition and underfive mortality is lower in Kerala because of more equitable distribution of food between income groups and within families and better access to and utilisation of health care facilities.

However, in Uttar Pradesh, Madhya Pradesh and Orissa, under-nutrition and under-five mortality rates are higher, in spite of higher average dietary intake, because of the lack of equitable distribution of food and access to health care. Identification and appropriate nutrition and health interventions among 'at risk' groups and under-nourished children are essential for optimal results. Equally important are interventions from related sectors to provide safe drinking water and improve environmental sanitation so that morbidity due to infections is reduced.

In spite of high per capita income, dietary intake and access to health care, both under-nutrition and infant mortality rates (IMR) are relatively high in Punjab. It is imperative that health and nutrition programmes are coordinated to achieve optimal synergy between the two interventions so that there is improvement in the nutritional and health status in all states.

Nutrition-Fertility Interactions

The association between low birth weight, under-nutrition during infancy and childhood and high infant mortality on the one hand and high parity and low inter birth intervals on the other have been well documented by research studies. Currently, birth order of three or more form over 50 per cent of all births in Uttar Pradesh, Madhya Pradesh and Bihar. In Kerala and Tamil Nadu, birth order of three or more constitute less than 30 percent of all births. Efforts to meet all unmet needs for contraception in the poorly performing states in order to reduce the high order of births would indirectly have a beneficial effect on child nutritional status, especially in terms of reduction in severe grades of undernutrition.

Coordination between ICDS and health functionaries to achieve optimal synergy between the interventions is critical for improving the nutritional and health status of women. In the last two decades, there have been reports on the health status and growth performance of Indian children from the low-income group who have been adopted and grew up without nutritional constraints during childhood. Data from these studies suggest that these children have a substantially higher prevalence of obesity during childhood, adolescence and in adult life.

Girls have higher body weight and body fat and, compared to their counterparts, attain menarche one or two years earlier. This, in turn, may result in their being shorter than their counterparts as skeletal growth ceases after menarche. In view of the changing dietary habits and life styles and the increase in obesity, research studies may have to be taken up to document the growth pattern of Indian children living not only under nutritional constraints but also among affluent groups and their impact on adult stature and reproductive function.

Dietary Intake and Nutritional Status of Pre-School Children

Pre-school children constitute one of the most nutritionally vulnerable segment of the population and their nutritional status is considered to be a sensitive indicator of community health and nutrition. There has not been a substantial improvement in their energy intake over the last two decades (Table 11). However, there has been a reduction in moderate and severe under-nutrition. Though there has not been any improvement in micronutrient intake over the years, there has been a substantial decline in the prevalence of nutritional deficiency signs. This is, perhaps, because of the better access to health care and effective treatment of infections. The decline in fertility and reduction in the higher order births may also have contributed to this because prevalence of severe forms of undernutrition is higher among higher order births.

Table 11. Average Nutrient Intakes Among Pre-school Children

	1-3 years			4-6 years		
	1975-79	1988-90	1996-97	1975-79	1988-90	1996-97
Protein (g)	22.8	23.7	20.9	30.2	33.9	31.2
Energy (Kcal)	834	908	807	1118	1260	1213
Vitamil A (mg)	136	117	133	159	153	205
Thiamin(mg)	0.50	0.52	0.40	0.76	0.83	0.70
Riboflavin (mg)	0.38	0.37	0.40	0.48	0.52	0.60
Niacin (mg)	5.08	5.56	4.60	7.09	8.40	7.40
Vitamin C (mg)	15	14	15	20	23	25

Intra-familial Distribution of Food

It is widely believed that in India, especially among the rural poor, food distribution is not based on 'need'. The breadwinner gets sufficient food, the children get the next share and the women take the remains. In times of scarcity, the dietary intake of women and children are likely to be most adversely affected. Several small studies in different states have reported that intra-familial distribution of food follows this traditional pattern even today. However, this may not be applicable to all states and all strata of society.

Analysis of data from diet surveys carried out by the NNMB in 1975-79 and in 1996-97 using the 24 hours dietary recall method . Data from the repeat survey showed that there has been reduction in the proportion of families where both adults and pre-school children were having inadequate food intake. However, it is a matter of concern that the proportion of families where the dietary intake of adults is adequate but that of pre-school children is inadequate has nearly doubled. Nutrition and health education on child-feeding and child-rearing practices are of paramount importance in improving the dietary intake and nutritional status of children through appropriate intra-familial distribution of food.

Improving Nutritional Status of Pre-school Children

The ICDS scheme was initiated in 1975 with the following objectives:-

— to improve the health and nutrition status of children in the 0-6 age group by providing supplementary food and coordinating with state health departments to ensure the delivery of the required health inputs;

— to provide conditions necessary for pre-school children's psychological and social development through early stimulation and education;

— to provide pregnant and lactating women with food supplements;

— to enhance the mother's ability to provide proper child care through health and nutrition education;

— to achieve effective coordination of policy and implementation among the various departments to promote child development.

The initial geographic focus of ICDS was on drought-prone areas and blocks with a significant proportion of scheduled caste and scheduled tribe population. In 1975,

33 blocks were covered under ICDS. Over the last two decades the ICDS coverage has progressively increased. The nutrition component of the ICDS aims at providing food supplements to pre-school children between the age of six months to six years, pregnant and lactating mothers and adolescent girls.

The type of food supplements in the ICDS programme varies widely, from ready-to-eat food to the supply of supplements cooked in the anganwadi. The emphasis was initially on providing cooked food through on-the-spot feeding in the anganwadi because it was believed that

— this would ensure that the targeted child would get food supplements, which would not be shared between other members of the family; and

— the anganwadi centres would provide practical nutrition education to women on cooking and feeding young children.

However, the on-the-spot cooked food feeding programme has several disadvantages as well. They are:

— children especially those in the age group of 6-36 months cannot consume the entire amount of food provided because of a smaller stomach capacity;

— even if older children do eat the food provided in the anganwadis, this acts mainly as a substitute, and not an addition, to home food;

— the most needy segments viz., children in the critical 6- 36 month age group and women, may not be able to come to the anganwadis duty and receive the food;

— providing food supplements only to the children from BPL families or those with under-nutrition is not possible as it may be difficult to feed one child and withhold food from another in the same anganwadi;

— cooking food, feeding the children and cleaning the vessels and the anganwadi take up most of the time of the anganwadi workers and helpers, leaving them little time for other important activities such as growth monitoring, nutrition education, or pre-school education;

— in any mass cooking and feeding programme, the monotony of the food provided and relatively poor quality of the preparations is a problem;

— cooking in poor hygienic conditions and keeping left-over food may result in bacterial contamination of food;

— under-nourished children, even those in the 3-6 year age group, if given double rations, cannot consume all the food at one sitting in the anganwadi.

Evaluation of the ICDS Nutrition Component

The nutrition component of the programme was evaluated by the Nutrition Foundation of India (NFI), Delhi, National Institute of Public Cooperation and Child Development (NIPCCD), Delhi, and the National Council of Applied Economic Research (NCAER), Delhi. In addition, there have been several small-scale evaluations. There were major reviews of the nutrition sector and ICDS programme by the World Bank and the Government of India in 1997 and 2001. The findings showed:

— ICDS services were much in demand but there are problems in delivery, quality and coordination;

— the programme might be improving food security at the household level, but does not effectively address the issue of prevention, detection and management of the undernourished child/mother;

— children in the 6-36 months age group and pregnant and lactating women do not come to the anganwadi and do not get food supplements;

— available food is shared between mostly children in the 3-5 years age group irrespective of their nutritional status;

— as there was no attempt in ensuring that all children are weighed, the children with severe CED could not be identified and offered double the rations as envisaged in the ICDS guidelines. As a result, there is very little focussed attention on the correction of undernutrition, prevention and management of health problems associated with moderate and severe under-nutrition.

— child care and nutrition education of the mother is poor or non-existent.

— there were gaps in the training and knowledge of anganwadi workers. Also, supervision of the programme, community support and intersectoral coordination was poor.

Nutrition Component of PMGY

Under Pradhan Mantri Gramodhaya Yojna 15% funds are earmarked for Nutrition Component. As the funding for PMGY is through the Gadgil-Mukherjee formula, the populous poor states with high under-nutrition rates do not get sufficient funds. The Department of Women and Child Development implemented the nutrition component of the programme providing take-home food supplements to children in the 6-36 months age group in the first two years viz., 2000-01 and 2001-02. From 1st April 2002, the Planning Commission has taken over its implementation. Some of the available data indicate that in many states:

— there was difficulty in procuring locally available take-home food supplements;

— relatively expensive ready-to-eat food, and not cereal-pulse-oilseed mix was provided;

— the funds provided under the nutrition component of PMGY were not treated as an additionality but were substituted for state's own Plan funds for nutrition;

— there has not been any substantial improvement in the enrolment of children.

The guidelines laid down for the nutrition component of PMGY emphasise that all infants and children should be weighed at least once in three months to detect those who are under-nourished so that health and nutrition interventions could be undertaken. Even though growth monitoring is an essential component of ICDS, this actually has not been operationalised. During the Tenth Plan, the physical and financial evaluation and the impact of the programme on infant feeding practices or infant nutritional status will be taken up.

ICDS During the Tenth Plan

During the Tenth Plan, every effort will be made to strengthen India's commitment and institutional capacity to combat under-nutrition in pre-school children and pregnant and lactating women. The nutrition component of ICDS will be specifically directed to achieve reduction in both micro and macro-nutrient under-nutrition. The focus will be on:

— strengthening the nutrition and health education component so that there is appropriate intra-familial distribution of food based on needs;

— reaching children in the 6-36 months age group, pregnant and lactating women;

— weighing all vulnerable population, identify those with CED and provide integrated health and nutritional support so that they recover within the next three months;

— ensuring universal screening of all children at least once a quarter to identify those children with growth faltering;

— focusing health and nutrition intervention (by providing take-home supplements) to ensure that children in Grades III and IV under-nutrition are in Grade II by the next quarter;

— looking for and treating health problems associated with severe under-nutrition;

— enhancing the quality and impact of ICDS substantially through training, supervision of the ICDS personnel and improved community ownership of the programme;

— concentrating on the improvement of the quality of care and inter-sectoral coordination and strengthening nutrition action by the health sector;

— creating nutrition awareness through IEC at all levels (community, women's group, village-level workers, PRIs, programme managers and policy makers at the state and central levels);

— establishing a reliable monitoring and evaluation mechanism

There is a shift in focus from providing cooked food at anganwadis to take-home food supplementation (under the PMGY and the pilot project providing food-grains to under-nourished pregnant and lactating women and adolescent girls). Undoubtedly, the take-home food supplements provided will be shared with the family, but that would add to household food security. When coupled with nutrition education, the undernourished persons may get their due share.

Nutritional education and careful monitoring of weight of the under-nourished individual will go a long way in ensuring that the person does get her due share. This shift may free the anganwadi workers and helpers from the time-consuming task of cooking and cleaning, giving them time for their other designated tasks for child development. During the Tenth Plan, inter-sectoral linkages between the health and the ICDS programmes will be strengthened. The Health sector will :

— invest in upgrading the nutritional knowledge and skills of all health care workers;

— focus on the management of health problems in moderately and severely under-nourished children; and

— train health and anganwadi workers so that they provide nutrition and health education on feeding of infants and young children and nutrition counseling to parents with sick children.

Simultaneously, efforts will be made to build up institution capacity for strengthening

— advocacy for nutrition among policy makers, programme implementers, women's groups, PRIs etc;

— country's capacity for nutrition action, training and research; and

— the network of medical colleges, home science colleges, centres undertaking nutrition monitoring and nutrition education.

Priority areas for research in nutrition during the Tenth Plan will include:

— operational research to identify and eliminate constraints in the ongoing programme; and

— analysis of nutrition needs at the local level and tailoring ongoing nutritional interventions to meet these needs.

Mid-day Meal Programme

The National Programme of Nutritional Support to Primary Education commonly known as Mid Day Meals Scheme was launched in August, 1995 as a 100% centrally funded Centrally Sponsored Scheme. The objective of the programme is to give a boost to universalisation of Primary Education by increasing enrolment, retention and attendance and simultaneously improving nutritional status of students in primary classes.

5

Enhancing Electricity Access in Rural Areas

An estimated 1.64 billion people worldwide lack access to electricity, of which approximately 80% live in rural areas of South Asia and Sub-Saharan Africa. In India itself, only 31% of rural households have access to electricity as per the 1991 Census. This number has not changed substantially in the last decade and by all recent estimates, rural household electrification still stands at around 33% in India. Non-access to electricity and rural poverty are closely correlated. This is because not only is electricity a pre-requisite for ameliorating living standards, it is also an indispensable input for productive and economic activities.

For vulnerable rural populations, the positive impacts of electricity inputs for basic activities such as pumping water for drinking and irrigation; lighting for extending March 2003 working and learning hours; and powering small-scale rural industry are considerably greater due to a bundling of socio-economic benefits. For example, reduced labor time for obtaining electrically pumped and hygienic drinking water may potentially free up time for income generation activities by women, which may in turn be aided by electricity inputs.

The positive contribution of electricity to the Human Development Index is strongest for the first kilowatt-hour, reflecting that the poorest are most likely to benefit from even minimal electricity inputs. However, electricity supply to this category in particular should be enhanced keeping broader development goals in mind, such as health, education, and economic productivity. A range of multilateral discourse has taken cognizance of the relationship between affordability, accessibility, and availability of appropriate forms of electricity for the rural poor and achieving the Millenium Development Goals of eradicating extreme poverty.

Where extension of the grid is physically and economically unviable, however, meeting these goals is particularly complex. This is true for communities in remote locations with dispersed populations. Deprivation for this category is indeed multi-faceted: a lack of sufficient attention by government programs is compounded by a lack of access to infrastructure services, markets, and information. Moreover, experience in developing countries- particularly those of South Asia and Africa-has shown that where grid electricity is available, supply is often erratic and of poor quality. Where alternatives to the grid exist, such as SHS (solar home lighting systems) available at subsidized rates, the technology itself is unsustainable unless accompanied by effective follow-up servicing and maintenance support.

Yet another issue is that provision of electricity, particularly through off-grid renewable energy technologies (RETs), does little to significantly raise living standards unless it also enables income generation. Literature has also pointed to the crucial emerging lesson that productive uses of renewable energy requires much greater attention from donors, development agencies and governments. These and other commonly acknowledged issues are in fact just the beginning of the rural electrification problem in India. Given that electrification occurs within a macro-economic framework-which is increasingly being transformed through reforms and restructuring-a host of complexities enter the picture.

In developing countries such as India and many in Latin America and Africa, the pre-reform scenario is characterized by state-owned power utilities with a verticallyintegrated and monopolized business comprising generation, transmission, distribution and customer services. Such a monopoly has shown to suffer severe technical and nontechnical efficiency losses. Some of the chief drivers of electricity reform in the developing world have hence been identified as

— inherent weakness in the state-run electricity sector in terms of unmet financial targets and inadequate or unreliable service provision,

— paucity of funds to meet infrastructure and maintenance requirements, and

— excess expenditure on subsidies (that may not be reaching the target group).

Rural electrification in developing countries has also suffered due to financial constraints. Generally the responsibility of the government, public utilities are required to extend the grid to rural areas without having tariff structures or collection ability to recover service costs. This results in urban consumers or national funds subsidizing rural access.

In poorer countries, the physical factors make the fixed cost of transmission and distribution (T&D) particularly high for grid extension to a rural population. Since the population density and demand are typically low, the average cost is higher (fixed costs are divided between fewer people and fewer units). With strong support from multilateral development agencies such as the World Bank, the traditional model of state-owned power utilities in some developing countries has given way to restructuring, and in some cases, market competition for electricity.

In India, electricity sector reforms are underway primarily to restore efficiency and financial health in the sector. Plagued by inefficient technical and managerial practices, the vertically integrated state electricity boards (SEBs) are unable to meet growing demand and provide quality service. Further, cross-subsidies allowing for almost zerocost electricity to certain end-users, high T&D losses due to theft, and other drains have severely constrained the financial resources of the sector. After a failed attempt in the early 1990s to invite private participation in electricity generation, various states in India have begun to follow a largely common pattern of reforms, spearheaded by the World Bank-supported Orissa model in the mid-nineties. State-level reforms in India are hence marked by some or all of the following:

— unbundling into three separate sectors of generation, transmission, and distribution,

— corporatization of the units

– private sector participation in generation and distribution,

— tariff and subsidy restructuring, and

— establishment of an independent state electricity regulatory commission (SERC).

Added financial impetus to the reforms process came in the form of the renamed Accelerated Power Development and Reform Program (APDRP), in which states willing to undertake distribution reforms are eligible for drawing funds. It is not immediately apparent how these elements could affect rural access, although rural access through the grid may face more barriers under reforms.

Firstly, since reforms in India aim to refocus subsidies and rationalize tariffs, it is likely that rural customers will have to pay more for services. Secondly, with "return on investments" becoming a critical evaluation parameter for electrification projects under reforms, addressing the sheer magnitude of rural electricity deprivation may in fact become increasingly expensive. The poorest and most underprivileged sections of rural society may be entirely excluded from electrification plans, since an electricity industry that is attempting to increase its financial viability may tend to be biased towards urban areas.

Regulation would be required to ensure that access is increased and the rural poor segment of society is not shut out of the market. For rural areas it would be worthwhile to look at alternative technology options such as distributed generation and supply based on renewable sources of energy. It is important to note that other developing country experiences with reforms, notably Chile, have been successful in expanding access in rural areas in large part because alternative technologies were looked at very seriously.

Scope for off-grid renewables: Due to a number of government initiatives, distributed generation and supply using renewable sources may be increasingly favored in India. For example, the Electricity Bill 2001 recently passed by the Standing Committee on Energy is the first to make specific reference to renewable energy in the national electricity mix; off-grid systems for rural electrification; and the obligation to extend supply to rural areas. While clause 6 supports complete rural electrification by increasing the involvement of local stakeholders in the management of distribution, clause 4 speaks of the formulation of a policy "permitting stand alone systems including those based on renewable sources of energy (and other non-conventional sources of energy) for rural areas".

Various government targets may enhance the scope for off-grid renewables given that DG is more cost-effective than extending the grid in certain situations. Further, as more information is available on renewables, it is anticipated that their competitiveness in remote areas would gain wider recognition. The central question underlying these targets concerns the funding and other resources available for off-grid rural electrification. Funding opportunities have been announced at the national level.

For example, direct funds are now available both for grid extension and stand-alone power plants under the Prime Minister's Minimum Needs Program-PMGY (Pradhan Mantri Gramodaya Yojana). IREDA (Indian Renewable Energy Development Agency), MNES' financing arm, continues to provide subsidized interest rates and long repayment schedules to buyers of renewable energy devices. Subsidies, however, have gradually been decreasing due to a shift from direct financial incentives (i.e. subsidies) to indirect fiscal incentives (i.e. interest subsidies). In any case, such funds by themselves may not be effective unless accompanied by a clear strategy for implementation.

Electrification of Remote Villages

Although electrification statistics of most states are quite good, there are big gaps between this data and actual access to electricity. This is true not only for remote and inaccessible locations such as islands, hilly areas, and reserved forests; it is equally true for villages that are electrified as per records, but show very little semblance of being electrified. In order to understand the levels of deprivation, the degree of vulnerability of the population, and possible reason for their predicament, examples have been taken from TERI case studies from various regions in India.

Deprivation Levels

a) The first category of a deprived population is one that cannot afford the electricity services that come to it at a higher price than its neighbors due to its non-existence as per revenue records: This is on account of the fact that electrification plans are made and implemented for revenue villages only. A hamlet is neglected until it is recognized as a revenue village. In this context, a clarification from the erstwhile RSEB (Rajasthan State Electricity Board) states that for electrifying those hamlets that are located away from the main inhabited village, and where no electrification equipment currently exists, villagers are expected to pay extra charges calculated on the basis of actual expenditure that would be incurred for extending the low-tension (LT) line from the inhabited village upto the hamlet.

b) A situation where the consumers pay for what they do not get characterizes the second type of deprivation: This alarming situation arises due to poor supply and usage of electricity. Typically, a consumer in Sawai Madhopur has paid between Rs. 1,500 and 3,000 for the initial electricity connection, and another Rs. 1,000 for internal wiring and fixtures. The tariff rates are calculated based on fixed charge and energy charge rates (this example is from customers of Jaipur Vidyut Vitaran Nigam Ltd. (JVVNL)-one of three discoms in Rajasthan). The fixed charges are Rs. 50 if the consumption remains within 50 units, and Rs. 75 if it exceeds this. Energy rates are Rs.1.7 per unit for consumption upto the first 50 units, and Rs. 2.75 per unit for subsequent consumption.

Minimum billing amount in rural areas is Rs. 65 for the first 50 units and Rs. 90 subsequently. On an average, a consumer pays an electricity bill of Rs. 110-150 per month. The electricity services on the other hand are far from satisfactory, frequently characterized by blackouts and brownouts. According to these consumers, continuous power cuts to the tune of 16-20 hours for 20 days in a month are a common occurrence.

c) Yet another type of deprivation exists in regions where, by virtue of their physical location, provision of grid electricity is techno-commercially unviable, and in some cases, prohibited by forestry and biodiversity law: A typical example is Sagar Dweep, the largest and also the most prosperous island in the Sunderbans due to development of agriculture, introduction of commercial crops, and tourism. The population aspires for electricity for various domestic, community and commercial services. Being an island, extension of grid faces both technological and economical constraints.

Currently, electricity is being supplied by the West Bengal State Electricity Board for 4 hours a day using diesel generators. However, supply is limited to only 650 customers who are concentrated along the main artery road of the island. It is reported that the loss incurred by the WBSEB is about Rs. 2.5 lac per month for operating the diesel generator. Villages in and around Ranthambhore National Park and Karauli Wildlife Sanctuary are other examples of vulnerable communities.

d) Solar systems that can be used for domestic electricity supply are limited in their reach due to paucity of funds and lack of infrastructure, as their distribution is managed by the government under the central subsidy scheme. This category of deprivation is thus precipitated by the above wherein the population is eager to procure alternate technologies, but supply is inadequate

SHS either as the only source of improved lighting, or as a supplement to the grid during blackouts, has found many takers in both electrified and unelectrified areas. Broadly, the sale of these systems occurs under a target-oriented central subsidy scheme, which reduces the price of these systems to the customer by half. Typically, a system worth Rs. 12,000 is sold at Rs. 6,000. However, there are several other schemes at the state level that have piggy-backed on the central subsidy scheme to further bring down the price of the system to the user. The central subsidy scheme itself has undergone many changes.

Unfortunately, the non-uniform pricing structure sends twisted signals to the population, which waits in vain for the lowest PV system price. Further, these schemes are limited by funds and hence can serve only a part of the population, usually on a first-cum-first-serve basis. The rest of the aspiring population-sometimes within the same village-waits for the following scheme to be announced, which may never actually happen.

e) Households that have already invested in SHS now face a problem with respect to repair and maintenance. This represents yet another kind of deprivation: A graver concern has been due to unreliable repair and maintenance services for the SHS systems in remote and inaccessible regions, such as Uttaranchal. Due to difficult terrain and low density of systems, the services that are contracted by the state agencies to the supplier have been very poor.

Although most of the faults are minor in nature, such as the need for a fuse replacement, the user has to wait for the all too infrequent visit of the maintenance contractor for simple procedures. SHS that offer a technically viable and acceptable option for minimum electricity supply needs are hence unable to serve the population due to inadequate servicing infrastructure. Distribution schemes under which these systems were made available have ignored the requirement for enhancing local capacity that could very ably manage and sustain the systems.

Distributed Generation (DG) Option

DG includes the application of small modular power generating technologies (such as turbines and micro-turbines, renewables, and hybrids) typically in the range of 1 kW to 50 MW. These technologies can be combined with energy management and storage systems, and used to improve the operations of the electricity delivery systems at or near the end user. DG may or may not be connected to the main electricity grid. Renewables, as a distributed generation option, have a crucial role to play in achieving the objectives of the Village Electrification Programme for remote inaccessible villages, and the national objective of "Power for All" by 2012. However, there are unresolved issues pertaining to

— the extent to which renewables can fill the demand-supply gap that is created by the limitations of grid extension, and
— the facilitating mechanisms that are required to bring renewablesbased distributed generation and supply of electricity into the mainstream of rural electrification planning.

Broadly, these issues can be categorized under:

— Technology options and their techno-commercial viability
— Management and community involvement in planning and implementation
— Institutional requirements, including those embedded in regulatory and policy frameworks
— Funding and financial mechanisms

Distributed Generation and Electricity Supply

Distributed generation (DG), by way of setting up small generating units based on a variety of local energy sources with localized distribution, has been identified as one of the alternatives for ensuring supply of power in rural areas. In India, DG is not a recent phenomenon. Diesel-based stand-alone DG systems (gensets) are commonly used by individual shopkeepers and house owners to provide back-up power during power failure.

Large-scale power intensive industries and commercial buildings have also installed their own captive power plants. However, these are not sustainable systems. The use of diesel is not only costly to the nation's economy and energy security, it is also highly polluting. Therefore, the use of renewable energy or renewable hybrids, combined with advanced DG technologies, is likely to be favored over conventional DG.

DG is ideally suited to electrification of remote and inaccessible rural areas. By constituting a Committee on Distributed Generation under the aegis of Ministry of Power, the GoI has already accorded importance for promoting the use of DG under a designated program. The terms of reference of the Committee clearly lay emphasis on the potential for DG in the context of rural electrification. However, there has been no study as of yet on the types of DG technologies needed to actually spur the process of development.

It is likely that different levels of development would require different technologies and implementation schemes, suggesting the need for different DG options. In this chapter, the Rural Electricity Supply Technology (REST) mission, recently commissioned under the MoP, proposes to evolve a strategy based on technologies that could provide for low cost power generation and low cost delivery in rural areas. It is anticipated that these could be managed by local institutions like Village Panchayats and NGOs.

Renewables Based DG Schemes

Distributed generation is yet to be tried on a large scale in rural electrification projects. There are still many barriers-technical, financial, regulatory, and institutional-that need to be addressed adequately. In other words, a clear and well-established framework is required to design, implement, and mainstream such schemes. Although there are many technologies available for DG schemes that are mature and field-proven, the solution to electricity access does not lie in selecting the winning technological innovation alone, but also in developing mechanisms for effective delivery of its services.

To illustrate with an example, it is not merely adequate to setup a biomass gasifier-based minigrid in a village, it is equally important to tie-up biomass delivery systems, fool-proof metering and billing, effective consumer redressal, and supply of quality end-use appliances. Besides, there are issues related to technology development and customization itself that need to be taken up on a mission mode.

Some of the available and potential technologies (biomass gasifier for rural electrification in small (10 kW) capacity range) for DG are still to go through the developmental cycle before they can be exploited fully. It is obvious that in many cases the DG schemes may not be commercially viable and concessions may have to be given, particularly in the initial stages of setting up the scheme and in some cases where small-scale RETs for poor rural consumers may be concerned.

Even though the word "subsidy" has become unpopular in the reforms scenario, it cannot be outrightly rejected in view of the need to electrify low-demand, inaccessible rural areas. Concessions are beneficial if they encourage access, rather than cover the operating costs. Competitive bidding, concessions to local bodies, low household connection fee, among others, are some of the ways of administering subsidies and concessions that would encourage electricity service provision and its use.

It is not easy to find lenders to finance DG schemes that are based on new or relatively unknown technologies such as micro-turbines, fuel cells, or wind turbines. These technologies are perceived by the lenders to have high resource and technology transfer risks, especially those associated with uncharted rural areas. It is not easy to convince lenders to fund the cost of innovation and for being a trailblazer.

Further, due to resource and demand constraints, most of these schemes are small in size and have high transaction costs associated with them. From a lender's point of view, it takes a lot of time and effort for verification, monitoring and evaluation. There is also an element of risk associated with the uncertainties in government policies with respect to depreciation, tax credits, and subsidies on conventional options, which ultimately affect the viability of any DG scheme.

Investors may be reluctant to support off-grid DG schemes if there is a risk that an aggressive grid expansion plan may undermine the effort in the near future. Then there are regulatory issues that need to be addressed, particularly for gridconnected DG schemes. The DG schemes are site-specific in nature and hence it is difficult to apply rigid and uniform rules and regulations. For example, a DG scheme based on feeding wind-generated electricity to the grid may compete well in a region where it has the potential to replace the most expensive fuel in the conventional fuel mix. In fact, tariff calculations can play an important role in promoting DG schemes if they are based on comparing tariffs between the DG scheme and those based on delivered cost of grid electricity at site.

Further, while comparing the DG versus conventional option, considerations should also be made as to whether the plant load factor of the DG scheme will be lower at least in the initial stages as compared with its conventional counterpart. Uncertainty in availability of the natural resource (for a renewables-based DG scheme) and uncertainty in demand leading to surplus (or deficit) power is another typical risk that has to be borne by the DG scheme. Thus, policies regarding net-metering, third party sale, wheeling and banking of surplus power, along with others, play an important role in deciding the viability of the DG scheme. Sensitizing the regulator to enable him to appreciate such uncertainties and risks is an important area to be addressed.

An equally big challenge is to involve the local community at various stages of planning and implementation of the scheme. It is important to realize that different levels of rural development would require different DG technologies. This is also in view of the fact that the design and implementation of DG schemes are very sitespecific -often depending on the geographic and demographic details of the population, load pattern, availability of other infrastructure (roads, communications, repair facilities), and requirement for energy services.

DG Scheme Based on Small-scale RETs

Electricity provision and development are hence synchronized because the focus is on electricity services that are appropriately designed and attuned to developmental levels. While facilitating a required level of development, the scheme may in turn prepare the community for the next level, which may then be ready for the higher capacity DG scheme. A sequence may thus emerge where the DG scheme is categorized such that it starts from a fairly elementary scheme, namely small-scale household level RETs, and graduates to higher capacity DG (possibly through the establishment of mini power plants, each with their own distribution network), and finally integration of such mini power plants into a localized grid or into the main grid itself. Thus at each level, not only would the respective technologies be different, but the institutional arrangements and financing policies would also be adapted accordingly.

A majority of the population in small, isolated villages aspires for improved lighting, which could also be considered the first step towards development. Such a pattern of demand suggests that SHS are a viable option, at least for the short-term future of 3-5 years until some other option such as the renewable-diesel hybrid becomes technocommercially viable. Although India has one of the largest government-supported and subsidized SHS programs in the world-about 180,000 currently in use -it continues to face problems due to limited financial resources and outreach.

At the state level, the distribution schemes are not only limited by financial resources from the MNES, they are further restricted due to grossly inadequate field-level infrastructure, particularly for providing after-sales service. This is a major issue because not only is after-sales service needed for carrying out minor repair jobs, it may be the only source that isolated communities have for purchasing spare parts. Unless the local community and NGOs pitch in with some alternate delivery scheme-not only for one-time delivery of systems, but also for sustained after-sales service-the state energy development agency alone will never be able to service the vast unelectrified and poorly electrified communities that clearly see SHS as an alternative and often preferred option to electricity from the grid.

The involvement of local community and NGOs to develop local enterprises is one possible way to address the problem of wider dissemination of SHS-based DG scheme. This approach, however, does not address a more important barrier that is related to the high upfront cost of SPV technology. Some successful models across the world have shown that access to credit improves the purchasing conditions of the potential customer and they find it easier to buy a system on credit. While this may be true for a majority of the population in small isolated communities, there is still a sizable portion that cannot afford any modern device at any cost with their current livelihood conditions.

For such communities, availability of credit can only follow an initial phase in which their ability to repay the loan has been enhanced. Any DG scheme for this category of households has to be linked with an income generating activity. Thus, for villages in this category, a DG scheme for household electrification based on SHS needs to be designed not only for augmenting the supply of SHS in the region, but also for strengthening the distribution and after sales service chain by facilitating the development of local capabilities to assemble, supply, and service the systems. This type of DG is not only expected to facilitate enterprise development on the supply side, it could also potentially enhance livelihood activities that can be linked to the provision of electricity services.

Villages in this category require basic infrastructure for socio-economic development; SPV could be a facilitator for this development. The Barefoot College approach is a pioneering example in this direction. Three important factors thus emerge with respect to the household-level DG scheme: (i) supply should be augmented through an alternative delivery scheme where local community based groups and entrepreneurs could play an integral role, (ii) credit should be available for those interested in availing of the scheme, (iii) small-scale RETs should enable income generation.

DG Scheme Based on Off-grid Mini Power Plants

DG scheme based on off-grid mini power plants with localized distribution for a cluster of villages: The possible solutions to problems faced by a large village or village cluster lie in exploring DG options such as mini power plants with localized distribution network based on locally available resources, rather than extending the grid. Such a scheme could be ideal for a cluster of small villages similar to the above or a large village. In fact, having benefited from the initial stages of development that is facilitated by the earlier DG scheme, the small isolated communities may also be potential users for the higher capacity DG scheme.

The socio-economic significance of the DG scheme based on minigrids is much higher in remote and distant rural areas, forest areas, and islands as shown by the Sunderbans experience. The effectiveness of the chosen institutional and financial model for such a DG scheme is critical in deciding its success. Energy Service Companies (ESCOs) can play an important role in this type of DG scheme, although some incentives may be required in order to attract them to the rural electrification business. One-time capital subsidy on the plants and the assets is one such incentive. However, the mode of delivering such a concession could be through competitive bidding with special incentives to local enterprises and local bodies such as the village committee.

Further, an innovative approach is required to finance the DG scheme which may assume the form of a concessional equity, debt financing, and offer of guarantees to the enterprise that take up the DG scheme, among others. As far as institutional mechanisms are concerned, close cooperation with manufacturers, vendors, financial intermediaries, village-level bodies, and NGOs is crucial in the operation and management of such schemes. The case study of the pilot project on micro-privatization of power distribution through the formulation of Village Electricity Committees (VEC) in the state of Orissa in India has clearly shown that it is possible to improve the operational and commercial viability of the electrification scheme if the community is made an important stakeholder.

The VEC consists of consumers from the village with participation of field staff of the utility with an objective of facilitating a single point contact. In this case, the VEC is recognized by the distribution company to have quasi-judicial powers. At the first stage, the VEC acts as a Consumer Care Centre in the village and facilitates interaction, education, grievance redressal, bill distribution, metering, and cash collection. In the interim stage, a greater accountability is transferred to the VEC by making it aware of the inputs at the transformer level and actual billing being achieved.

Subsequently, the energy accounting is completely transferred to the VEC whereby it acts like a cooperative or electricity association: it will be billed on transformer reading as a bulk consumer and the entire responsibility of collection will be transferred to it. The experience of Orissa shows that the involvement of local communities can be very useful in improving the financial and institutional viability of the DG scheme. To summarize, some of the desirable components of the DG scheme based on minigrids are:

— Maximizing the local content on the demand side by integrating communities in planning, decision making, O&M, and ultimately in ownership;

— Introducing innovative business approaches on the supply side through fee-forservice schemes using pre-paid cards as an option;

— Ensuring the means to finance the project through a combination of well-targeted and designed subsidies to take care of high up-front costs of rural electrification projects, and regular availability of microcredit to beneficiaries for starting income generation activities that will facilitate payment for services;

— Institutional strengthening by setting up appropriate linkages for generation, sale, and supply of electricity; and

— Capacity building and enhancement of all stakeholders to deliver and utilize the electricity services.

Although off-grid mini power plants facilitate greater community welfare and economic development as compared to the household-level schemes, they are still constrained by factors such as limited power supply (particularly with RET-based schemes), low load factor, limited opportunities for innovative financing available for the infrastructural sector, and other market-based business approaches. In order to improve their techno-commercial viability, integration of several off-grid DG schemes into a localized grid or the main grid network could be one option. Such interconnection would not only feed the surplus power to the grid, it would also strengthen the grid network.

DG Scheme Based on Integration of Local Minigrids

Some of the DG technologies such as wind turbines and biomass cogeneration systems feed electricity to high-voltage transmission systems. However, a small DG unit, typically of less than 10 MW capacity, can instead be connected to the low-voltage local distribution network or installed on buildings. Significant advantages of such a scheme is to improve the supply of electricity by reducing the load on the local systems through on-site generation, and by improving the voltage at the end of the village distribution systems.

DG options that feed into the main grid network have been tried and tested in urban situations in India. For example SPV power plants have been installed on the roof of urban buildings, particularly on commercial buildings. These schemes are meant for peak load shaving of the power demand curve, and are typically designed to meet the partial load of the building during peak demand. It can also feed power to the grid during holidays when building electricity requirements are low.

In India so far, 26 such schemes are operational in the country with their aggregate capacity at 1.9 MWp. In a country like India where reliability in the supply of power is one of the main concerns of rural electrification, a scheme involving small PV-based micro power plants for voltage support at remote sections of the weak grid, has been found to be quite useful. Such a scheme would be highly applicable in a remote (particularly mountainous) rural situation-both for providing power to the local community and for strengthening the local distribution network.

Typical plant size is in the range of 25-100 kWp. Another useful scheme is to promote small hydroelectric projects of upto 25 MW capacity each that are connected to the grid network. Similar projects based on biomass power have also been promoted. Such plants are ideal for supplying power to remote communities and for feeding extra power to the grid. Integration of minigrids into the localized grid or with the main grid network is a desirable state because it not only improves the economics of rural electrification, it also becomes amenable to market driven business approaches. Such a scenario ideally envisages a number of independent power producers competing in a subsidy-free and adequately regulated rural electricity market, with increasing the number of consumers being a key profit motive.

6 Communication

Postal System

An efficient postal system is crucial for growth and modernisation and it is fast emerging as an important component of the modern communication and information technology sector. The Indian postal system is the largest in the world, with a network of about 1.55 lakh post offices. Besides providing a variety of postal services, the Indian postal system also plays a crucial role in resource mobilisation, especially in the rural areas, which is illustrated by fact that deposits to the tune of Rs. 2,18,695 the crore had been mobilised as on 31 March 2001.

Review of Ninth Plan

The two major thrust areas of the Ninth Plan were expansion of postal services in the uncovered areas especially remote and rural areas and modernisation of the postal operations. Technology upgradation was accorded the highest priority for the first time under the Five-Year Plans, 58 per cent of the total approved outlay of the Ninth Plan being allocated for this purpose. The major areas covered during the Ninth Plan were:

— Expansion of the scope and coverage of the programmes of modernisation initiated during the

Eighth Plan period through the induction of new technology.

— Development and marketing of new services, especially those for the business/ professional sectors and modernisation of identified agency functions.

— Human resource development through appropriate training for upgrading skills.

— Streamlining of management functions.

— Development and maintenance of appropriate buildings for the modernised systems and staff quarters for the employees.

— Extending basic counter facilities in new areas in a cost-effective manner.

The physical targets are likely to be achieved, since performance on this front has been satisfactory. Against the target of setting up 250 permanent post offices, 253 are likely to be set up. Nearly 90 per cent of the target of 2,500 offices in rural areas is likely to be achieved. In addition, 4,691 Panchayat Sanchar Sewa Kendras (PSSKs) are likely to be opened during the Ninth Plan. The performance on the modernisation front has also been very encouraging, as 5,701 Multi-Purpose Counter Machines (MPCMs) are projected to be installed against the target of 5,000 and 150 V-SATs (very small aperture terminals) are projected to be installed against the target of 170.

An outlay of Rs. 507.25 crore was approved for the postal sector in the Ninth Plan for implementing various programmes. On the basis of allocations approved for the Annual Plans (BE), the operational approved outlay for the Ninth Plan works out to Rs. 545 crore. On the basis of actual allocation of funds, the operational outlay works out to Rs. 483.16 crore. As against this, the utilisation during the Plan is projected to be Rs. 408.91 crore. This works out to a utilisation ratio of 75 per cent of the approved operational outlay, 84 per cent of actual allocation and 80 per cent of the Ninth Plan approved outlay. The low utilisation is basically the result of reduced allocations at the RE stage from year to year.

The Ninth Plan also marked the beginning of diversification efforts by the Department keeping in tune with the times and with a view to generating more revenues. The diversification efforts are mainly in the form of introduction of premium products like express parcels, financial services like international money transfer and providing agency functions for mutual funds and other financial institutions and information technology (IT) products like e-post.

Challenges and Policy Reforms

Postal finances have deteriorated sharply over the last decade. Postal deficit is an openended subsidy and forms part of the general budget. The deficit has shot up almost 16 times, from Rs. 91.81 crore in 1992-93 to Rs.1,576.35 crore in 2000-01 (Table1). This has serious implications for resource availability for other needy sectors like infrastructure and social development.

Table 1. Trend of Postal Deficit

(Rs. crore)

Year	Deficit
1992-93	91.81
1997-98	993.43
1998-99	1,590.97
1999-2000(RE)	1,740.53
2000-01 (RE)	1,576.35
2001-02 (BE)	1,458.37

This situation cannot be sustained for long without serious implications. The Department should endeavour to achieve self-sufficiency over the next five years. This should be done through a twopronged strategy of increasing revenue and reducing costs. The first can be achieved through diversification and aligning postal tariffs to costs. Cost reduction can be effected through upgradation and modernisation of technology and redeployment/ reduction of manpower.

Postal services in India have been highly subsidised, as part of Government policy. While subsidy on a few items covered under the Universal Postal Service Obligation (UPSO) may be justified, the pricing of other services needs to be done on cost basis, taking into account what the market can bear. The details of per unit subsidy and the total amount paid on various services is in Table 2.

Table 2. Subsidy on Postal Services (Projections - 2001-02)

Service	Subsidy per unit (paise)	Traffic (in lakh)	Total deficit (Rs. crore)
Post Card	555.39	3,185.50	176.92
Printed post cards	381.33	1,214.50	46.31
Letter Cards	378.44	4,599.50	174.06
Registration	1,809.43	2,679.50	484.84
Money Order	2,894.35	1,105.00	319.83
Reg. Newspaper (S)	786.86	1,045.50	82.27
Reg. Newspaper (B)	1,283.25	174.50	22.39
Printed Books	1,110.73	322.00	35.77
Parcel	722.90	684.90	49.95
Others	-	13,159.50	33.09
Total	-	28,169.50	1,424.93

There does not seem to be any justification for subsidising services like registration, newspapers, postal orders, money orders, etc. Of the 23 services being provided by the Department, only Insurance, Speed Post and Foreign Mail are yielding a surplus. This policy of blanket subsidy needs to be reviewed and replaced by a policy of pricing the services appropriately, keeping the UPSO in mind. The tariff of non-UPSO services should be fixed on commercial principles and revised from time to time.

As a member of the Universal Postal Union, India is committed to ensure the provision of quality postal services on a regular basis to all the users at all points in the country at affordable prices. However, as per the Beijing Congress of Universal Postal Union (UPU) 1999, each country is to define the scope of its Universal Postal Service in line with the technical, economical and social environment as well as the needs of the customers. Keeping in mind our specific needs and in line with international conventions, the UPSO for India needs to be clearly defined and adopted. Taking into account the importance of the money order economy in the country, the UPSO needs to include money orders besides post cards, inland letters and envelopes. These services should continue to be delivered at affordable prices. The prices of other services should be determined on a commercial basis with a view to achieving self-sufficiency.

Under the Indian Postal Act, 1898, the Central Government fixes the tariffs for various postal articles and these are approved by Parliament. Due to various reasons, including political considerations, tariffs have not been revised at reasonable intervals. Revision of postal tariffs has not been keeping pace with the increase in operational costs. The present system of tariff fixation needs to be replaced by a more dynamic, objective and transparent mechanism. An independent regulatory mechanism needs to be created which, besides other things, would look after tariff fixation.

The Indian Post Office Act, 1898 is totally archaic and obsolete and does not meet the requirements of changed circumstances. It needs to be replaced with a forward-looking legislation to take care of new developments, including the emerging scenario of convergence, the new technological and other developments and competition.

The present scheme of opening rural post offices, i.e. EDBOs, has a large element of in-built subsidy of 67 per cent in normal areas and 85 per cent in hilly and tribal areas. This is not sustainable in the long run. Besides, the agents under the scheme tend to demand being given the status of permanent Government employees. If this is agreed to, it will put a tremendous strain on the financial system. The scheme needs to be replaced by an innovative programme of providing services in the rural areas. Two feasible options that must be explored are converting extra departmental employees into franchisees of the Department for providing postal services in rural areas and reactivating the scheme of licensed postal agents.

The first option may also help in reducing the financial burden and future liabilities of the Department in a major way, besides providing it with a decentralised system of privately-run and owned convergence centres at the village level. Reach and trust are the two very strong and unique advantages of the postal network in India. With the help of innovative strategies, this can be converted into a major advantage for the delivery of a variety of services, apart from postal services, in order to achieve self-sufficiency. To take advantage of the emerging scenario of convergence, post offices need to be developed as multiproduct and multi-service delivery centres in which delivery of postal services would only be a part of the job. It would involve the introduction of new value-added services, financial IT-based products, e-commerce and new postal products.

These convergence centres, as privately owned and operated outlets of franchisees of the Department, will have the potential of ushering in a new communications and financial services revolution in the rural and semi-urban areas. Generation of substantial additional revenue through non-tariff methods like commercial exploitation of land and introduction of IT based financial services are the two other important components of the strategy for making the Government run postal services self-financing.

A corporate set-up provides two intrinsic advantages - faster decision-making and raising resources from the market. In view of this, corporatisation of the postal network of the Department of Posts in a time-bound manner becomes imperative. The Financial Directorate envisaged to be set up on the pattern of Business Development Directorate of the Department of Posts should be converted into a corporation during the Tenth Plan as a step in this direction.

Except courier services, the postal services are still a State monopoly. To ensure efficiency and improve quality of service, it may be desirable to open up selected postal services to private entrepreneurs. This will ensure flow of required funds into the sector, bring in new technology and also enable the Department to pay greater attention to its main activity i.e. carrying of mail. To ensure competition and a level playing field, the establishment of an independent regulatory authority may be considered.

Postal systems the world over are increasingly becoming self-financing. They are run on commercial basis, taking due care of the UPSO, by independent corporate entities. The Indian postal system also needs to be reformed and made self-financing in line with global trends and in keeping with the country's needs.

Objectives and Targets of the Tenth Plan

In order to achieve the aim of financial selfsufficiency within the Tenth Plan period, a road map of specific measures needs to be drawn up and implemented. The major objectives envisaged for Tenth Plan are:

— Provision of universal postal services at affordable prices.

— Ensuring quality of services at par with international standards.

— Modernisation and process re-engineering with a view to achieving better administrative efficiency and financial management.

— Upgrading existing infrastructure to reduce cost of operation and enhance customer satisfaction.

— Making the postal operations of the Department self-financing by the end of the Plan period.

Some of the major targets for the Tenth Plan envisaged are:

— Opening of 100 departmental post offices.

— Computerisation of all major post offices.

— Computerisation of 136 Computerised

Registration Centres (CRCs) 506 Divisional Offices and 611 Costumer Care Centres.

— Setting up of a National Data Centre.

— Improving ergonomics in 10,000 post offices.

— Provision of infrastructure equipment to 45,448 rural post offices.

— Installation of additional Automatic Mail Processing Systems

Major Initiatives Envisaged for the Tenth Plan

Computerisation and connectivity has been identified as the core activity for the Tenth Plan. Coupled with the modernisation and mechanisation programme, the technology upgradation component constitutes the bulk of the outlay proposed for the Tenth Plan. The other major initiatives include expansion of the postal network, business development and financial services. The salient features and major issues concerning the major initiatives proposed for the Tenth Plan are:

Expansion of the Postal Network

It is proposed to open 100 permanent departmental offices and another 6,000 offices/ outlets through the existing schemes PSSKs and EDPOs. The EDBO and PSSK schemes involve a large amount of subsidy. The present policy of opening post offices in the rural areas needs to be replaced with innovative methods of providing these services like franchising arrangements. Keeping the overall goal of making the Department selffinancing in mind, no more post offices should be permitted to be opened in the rural areas under the present scheme.

Computerisation and Connectivity

The various schemes proposed for computerisation and connectivity relate to creating the basic infrastructure for improving the quality of existing services and providing the technological base for the launch of new value-added and financial services. Networking of various post offices, record offices, back offices, customer care centres, etc. forms an integral part of the entire programme. IT-based services are an important part of the product-mix envisaged to be delivered by the post offices in the Tenth Plan. The introduction of new services proposed may not be feasible without the required technological back up. Under this programme, the single most important activity proposed is complete computerisation and networking of 13,361 post offices.

A beginning in computerisation and modernisation was made in a small way in the Ninth Plan, based on the limited resources available. As a result, the Department could introduce new value-added services like express parcels, e-post and satellite money orders etc. The programme is envisaged on a much larger scale in the Tenth Plan, for which a substantial increase in the outlay for the Department has been provided. This would enable the Department to launch new services and improve the quality and efficiency of existing services and would go a long way in helping the Department become self-sufficient through substantial addition in resource generation.

Business Development

The programme aims at giving a new thrust to and expansion of the existing postal services like speed post, express parcels, e-post and introduction of new products like E-billing Payment and Presentment (EBPP), e-commerce etc.The separate Business Development Directorate with due delegated authority and powers, set up in the Department during the Ninth Plan for the promotion of these products, needs to be strengthened.

The Directorate has shown very encouraging results in promoting premium services. The revenue generated by the Directorate increased from Rs. 40 crore in 1994-95 to Rs. 281 crore in 2000-01. With the introduction of new products backed by required technological support, the revenue is expected to increase manifold in the Tenth Plan. The revenue projections for the Tenth Plan are given in Table 3.

Table 3. Revenue Projections - Premium Products

(Rs. crore)

Year	Revenue
2002-03	553
2003-04	774
2004-05	1,083
2005-06	1,517
2006-07	2,124

The country-wide reach of the Department extending to the remotest corners of the rural areas, is a rare asset which needs to be exploited fully for the delivery of various services. Revenue generation from these services would contribute in a big way to reducing the revenue deficit of the Department. The programme needs to be strengthened keeping in view the target of making the Department self-financing.

Financial Services

Introduction of smart cards and installation of ATMs (automated teller machines) in collaboration with the corporate sector are the other major new initiatives envisaged for the Tenth Plan. The quality of service of the existing products and their reach is envisaged to be further strengthened during the Plan period. The programme needs to be emphasised keeping in view the existing infrastructure and reach of the Department and the potential of generating substantial revenue.

Path Ahead

The Tenth Plan would endeavour to transform the postal system into a modern, efficient and self-financing set-up. To achieve this , the major initiatives/action points envisaged for the Tenth Plan are :

(i) Identification and adoption of UPSO and delivering the the items thereof at affordable prices.

(ii) Pricing of non-UPSO items to be determined on commercial basis.

(iii) Setting up of an independent regulatory body, which besides other things, would take care of tariff fixation.

(iv) Fresh post offices in locations are to be opened only through redeployment of staff. No additional posts are to be created for this purpose.

(v) A comprehensive review of all existing post offices is to be carried out in a time-bound manner and all units which do not fulfill the norms and where resources are underutilised need to be relocated.

(vi) A contributory pension scheme needs to be worked out to encourage extra departmental employees to become franchisees of the Department.

(vii) Post offices will have to act as multiproduct/ multi-service centres and convergence of services is to be the governing criterion.

(viii) Computerisation, connectivity and networking of the postal network are to be the cornerstones of Plan activity during the Tenth Plan.

(ix) The Indian Post Office Act, 1898, is to be replaced by a forward-looking legislation to take care of the needs of competition, convergence and other new developments.

(x) Develop and evolve a credible road map of corporatisation for the postal sector as India Post within the Tenth Plan.

(xi) An outlay of Rs. 1,100 crore was initially approved for implementing the various programmes/projects during the Tenth Plan. The outlay has been increased to Rs. 1,350 crore to adequately meet the requirement of funds for the core activity of computerisation and connectivity. The Schemewise breakup of this Tenth Plan outlay is given in the Appendix.

Telecommunications

Telecommunications is one of the prime support services needed for rapid growth and modernisation of various sectors of the economy. It has become especially important in recent years because of enormous growth of Information Technology (IT) and its significant impact on the rest of the economy. India is perceived to have a special comparative advantage in IT and in IT-enabled services. However, sustaining this advantage depends critically on high quality telecommunication infrastructure.

Keeping this in view, the focus of Tenth Plan has to be on the provision of world class telecommunication facilities at reasonable rates. Provision of telecom services in rural areas would be another thrust area to attain the goal of accelerated economic development and social change. Although the telecom network has grown rapidly in recent years, its growth needs to be accelerated further in the Tenth Plan. It is equally important to speed up structural changes in this sector in line with trends in other countries to ensure that telecommunication services are not only made available on the scale needed to sustain rapid growth in the economy as a whole but also that their cost are in tune with the expectations of a modernising economy.

For a dynamic sector, reforms is a continuous process necessitated by dynamics of change including technological innovations. The telecom sector in India has been witnessing a continuous process of reforms since 1991. With the opening of international long distance services and internet telephony from April, 2002, the process of liberalisation and opening up the sector for competition is complete. Convergence of services is a major new emerging area and the telecom sector will have to address this in the Tenth Plan.

The New Telecom Policy (NTP) announced in 1999 modified the NTP, 1994 to take into account the far-reaching technological developments taking place in the telecom sector globally and to implement the Government's resolve to make India a global IT superpower. NTP, 1999 also seeks to solve problems arising out of the implementation of NTP, 1994. The objectives of the NTP 1999 are to:

— Make available affordable and effective communications for the citizens.

— Strive to provide a balance between the provision of universal service to all uncovered areas, including the rural areas and the provision of high-level services capable of meeting the needs of the country's economy.

— Encourage the development of telecommunication facilities in remote, hilly and tribal areas of the country.

— Create a modern and efficient telecommunications infrastructure taking into account the convergence of IT, media, telecom and consumer electronics and thereby propel India into becoming an IT superpower.

— Convert Public Call Offices (PCOs), wherever justified, into Public Teleinfo centres offering multimedia services like Intergrated Service Digital Network (ISDN) services, remote database access, government and community information systems etc.

— Transform in a time bound manner, the telecommunications sector to a greater competitive environment in both urban and rural areas providing equal opportunities and level playing field for all players.

— Strengthen research and development (R&D) efforts in the country and provide an impetus to build world-class manufacturing capabilities.

— Achieve efficiency and transparency in spectrum management.

— Protect the defence and security interests of the country.

— Enable Indian telecom companies to become truly global players.

Ninth Plan Review

During the Ninth Plan period, a record growth rate of telecom services was achieved in the country. The network (equipped capacity) grew at an average rate of about 22 per cent. Growth of both cellular mobile phones and fixed line phones has been equally impressive. While private sector concentrated in cellular mobile phones segment, the growth in the Government sector was primarily due to fixed line connections. Against the target of providing 237 lakh Direct Exchange Lines (DELs), about 240.55 lakh additional DELs have been provided during the Ninth Plan. The cellular network has grown from a small base of 3.40 lakh connections to 64.31 lakh connections by the Plan end. As a result of this growth, the tele-density has nearly tripled from 1.57 at the beginning of the Ninth Plan to 4.4 as on March 31, 2002. Details in this regard are given in the Table 4:

Table 4. Network Expansion – Ninth Plan

(Lines in lakh)

	As on 31.3.1997	Net Addition– Public	Private	Ninth Plan Total	As on 31.3.2002	CAGR %
Fixed	145.40	234.68	5.87	240.55	385.95	21.56
Cellular	3.40	2.14	58.77	60.91	64.31	80.00
Total	148.80	236.82	64.64	301.46	450.26	24.79
Tele-density	1.57	-	-	-	4.4	-
VPTs	2.61	2.061	0.00846	2.07	4.68	12.39

The performance of the Public sector units, i.e. Bharat Sanchar Nigam Ltd. (BSNL) and Mahanagar Telephone Nigam Ltd. (MTNL), has been impressive. Against the target of installing 185 lakh new connections in the original Plan (which was revised to 222.7 lakh in Mid-Term appraisal for BSNL and MTNL and 237 lakh for the whole sector including private sector) the achievement during the Ninth Plan is 240.55 lakh connections including contribution of private sector i.e. more than the target envisaged in the Ninth Plan Document. Ninth Plan also witnessed the beginning of cellular services by the public sector. MTNL launched its mobile services in Delhi and Mumbai as the third operator.

The performance of the private sector during the Ninth Plan has been a mixed one. While it did very well in the expansion of cellular network, the performance was not encouraging in the fixed line segment. Only about 5.9 lakh DELs have been installed against the target of 52 lakhs(original) and the revised target of 14.3 lakh. Constraints like licensing agreements, unrealistically higher licence fees, revenue share, right of way etc. have been basically responsible for the slow progress for the private sector.

For the Government sector, an outlay of Rs.46,442.04 crore was approved for the Ninth Plan to be financed basically from internal and extra budgetary resources (IEBR). This included a small budget support component of Rs.44.04 crore meant for financing the Plan outlay of regulatory bodies like TRAI and Wireless Monitoring Organisation (WMO) etc. The approved outlay for the Ninth Plan was only indicative in nature and the Annual Plan outlays were to be fixed on the basis of resources that might become available during the year. The operational outlay for the Ninth Plan on the basis of the Annual Plan outlays approved on a year to year basis works out to Rs.84,783.90 crore including a budget support of Rs.208.20 crore.

As against this, plan expenditure is expected to be Rs.69,407.62 crore. This gives a utilisation of 163 per cent of the originally approved outlay and 89 per cent of the approved operational outlay. The shortfall in expenditure in comparison to the operational outlay was basically on account of lower expenditure by MTNL and BSNL due to delays in taking up some new projects and reduction in cost of equipment. On the financing side, the IEBR generation was lower than targeted (compared to operational outlay) basically on account of reduced requirement for market borrowings.The shortfall in internal resources generation by BSNL and MTNL could partly be attributed to tariff re-balancing.

Present Status of Telecom Network

The basic telecom services network has expanded from about 84 thousand connections at the time of independence to about 385.95 lakh working connections as on March 31 2002. Basic services network constitutes the bulk of the phones accounting for about 86 per cent of the total telecom network.

Challenges for The Tenth Plan

With the introduction of competition in the market, the focus of planning needs to shift from the overall expansion of DELs and network to providing requisite policy framework for the sector/ market to grow as required and consistent with the overall policy objectives. In determining the appropriate policy initiatives and the relevant regulatory framework for this purpose, we need to bear certain factors in mind.

Telecommunications is one of the fastest growing sectors in India. However, viewed in the context of global growth patterns and indicators, the sector is still in the early stages of development. Our tele-density was only 4.01 as compared to the global average of 32.78 (December, 2001) and 24.98 achieved by China. The status of teledensity along with other indicators like per capita income, number of PCs, Internet users etc.

The sector also needs, especially in terms of broadband, to expand at substantially higher rates to meet the needs of related sectors like IT, I & B and other sectors of the economy. Keeping this perspective in view, the sector needs to be treated essentially as an infrastructure sector for the next decade or so. Once the required tele-density is achieved and the necessary support network has been created, the sector could be treated as service sector.

With a view to ensuring optimum growth in the coming years, Government's broad policy of taxes and regulation for the telecom sector has to be a promotional one. Mopping up of resources or revenue generation by the Government should not be a determinant of the policy governing the sector. The incidence of licence fees in the form revenue share and spectrum charges has to be guided by this principle. Keeping in line with the policy adopted by most of the progressive administrations in the world, the licence fee need to be aligned to the cost of regulation and administration of Universal Service Obligations (USO).

As part of the promotional policy, there is need for the TRAI to work out afresh the revenue share and USO regime. The presence of multiple operators in various sectors implies a need to focus on the conditions that will enable these operators to function smoothly. Specific planning would be required to prepare the grounds for a multi-operator system to develop and the subscriber base to expand without impediments. Ensuring fair and timely interconnection is a major part of such an endeavour.

At present, a major obstacle to interconnection arises if the incumbent has to increase capacity to give interconnection and the demand for interconnection takes up only a small portion of the installed capacity. In such a situation, the incumbent finds it difficult to provide adequate funds to install the required capacity since it would not generate adequate payment to cover costs. Such a situation would merit Government intervention and it would be appropriate to establish a Fund that will help meet the cost of installing the capacity in such situations of inadequate demand. The Government may recover the amount funded over a period of time.

The Radio Frequency (RF) spectrum is a scarce natural resource. In accordance with international treaties, it has to be shared among a very large number of radio communication services and users - defence, civil, Government and private - based on the principles of co-existence and most efficient use. The increasing share of cellular mobile in total number of telephones points to a need for greater focus on the policy for allocating frequency spectrum. In addition to cellular mobile phones, which will have a large number of lines by the end of the Tenth Plan, frequency spectrum will be required also for the WLL used for providing basic services.

The advent of new technology will also pose a significant challenge for the planners of radio spectrum. The increasing adoption of wireless technologies and the need to align with international standards would mean that there will be a need to address the shortage of wireless spectrum and to reconcile competing demands in certain frequency bands. The policy governing spectrum allocation and licencing has to be so designed that this scarce resource is used optimally and does not become a constraint for growth.

The existence of an independent and effective regulatory body is crucial for ensuring optimum growth and free and fair competition. The independence of the regulator depends, to a large extent, on the funding mechanism, the constitution of the regulatory body and the principles guiding its functioning. Against the present system of funding from the budget support, a mechanism for making the regulatory body self-financing needs to be put in place. One such option could be provision of necessary funds out of levies/fees collected from telecom operators. Ensuring stability and clarity of regulatory principles are equally important for making the regulatory mechanism effective.

To ensure efficient functioning of the regulatory body, two crucial inputs are continuous upgradation of the skills of its staff and regular flow of all relevant information, including the one relating to latest technological developments. A structured approach needs to be developed to achieve these objectives. Besides ensuring that the competent personnel are attracted by the regulator, adequate training facilities and a framework of research and information service need to be developed. A team of research institutes could be identified for specific tasks in this regard. The Planning Commission itself could be a part of such a network.

Convergence of services is leading to a paradigm shift in the service composition, the structure of the industry and the way markets are organised. This is expected to lead to optimum utilisation of resources and provision of services on least cost basis. Service segmentation and separate license for each category/ service becomes redundant and work only as artificial barrier. These need to be removed by issuing a common or single licence for all telecom services and evolving common revenue share formula. Hence, the system of multiple licenses will have to give way to a single licence regime. This would mean having perfect competition across the country in services and among operators. The Communications Convergence Bill is expected to provide the basic framework for convergence of services.

Table 5. Telecom Development - International Comparison (As on December, 2001)

Country	Population (In crore)	GDP per capita (US$)*	DELs (Fixed) (In lakh lines)	Cellphones (In lakh lines)	Total Phones (In lakh lines)	Tele-density
USA	28.59	36211	1900.00	1270	3170.00	110.88
UK	6.01	23694	353.26	470.26	823.52	137.02
Australia	1.93	19897	100.60	111.69	212.29	109.99
Brazil	17.18	3500	374.31	287.46	661.77	38.52
Mexico	10.04	5807	137.73	217.57	355.30	35.39
S.Africa	4.38	2882	49.69	91.97	141.66	32.36
Egypt	6.46	1424	66.50	27.94	94.44	14.63
Japan	12.73	34337	760.00	748.19	1508.19	118.45
Malaysia	2.38	3838	47.38	71.28	118.66	49.86
China	129.61	834	1790.34	1448.12	3238.46	24.98
Pakistan	14.50	425	34.00	8.00	42.00	2.90
India	102.70	455	347.32	64.31	411.63	4.01
Asia	360.67	2354	3911.79	3366.14	7277.93	20.17
World	607.91	5274	10460.88	9462.97	19923.85	32.78

The Bill provides for different categories of licences viz. infrastructure facilities, networking services, network application services, content application services and valueadded network application services. Under the Bill, the designated authority will be able to decide as to how licensing is to be done when a particular operator wants to cover more than one category of licences The envisaged Authority may, while granting a license for any other categories confine or limit the scope of the facilities or services to be provided by the licensee in each category of licence and also specify the conditions for providing that facility or service.

Basic objective of this approach is to tackle the communications scenario appropriately in a layered manner. The Bill is expected to ensure seamless migration to the convergence regime and the operators shall not be asked to start all over again to revalidate the licences issued by DoT. Technology restrictions are not the best way to ensure compliance to the terms and conditions of any licence. Compliance needs to be ensured through more efficient and effective means which may include imposition of well defined penalties and cancellation of licences in critical cases. With a view to ensuring optimum growth and service provision on least cost basis, the licence must be technology neutral.

The existing policy should not be allowed to hold back the benefits accruing from technological innovations if it is not against the interest of the nation and the consumer. The benefits of internet telephony may be allowed to flow freely to anyone having the resources to establish access and may not be restricted to be channeled through ISPs. Similarly, the immense potential of WLL technology in the fast roll-out of services and its cost effectiveness need to be fully exploited in taking the services to rural areas in a time-bound and affordable manner. Various restrictions on its use especially for rural networks need to be removed immediately.

As WLL based services are basically in the nature of basic services, the concept of floor pricing (rentals) seems unwarranted and is against the basic spirit of competition, efficiency, affordability and consumer welfare. Though about 70 per cent of India lives in the villages and rural areas account for about 30per cent of the GDP, the development of telecom facilities in these areas is far from satisfactory. The tele-density in rural areas is only 1.14 against 10.16 in the urban areas. Viewed from the general accessibility point of view also, about one-third of the total villages in the country are yet to be connected by basic telecom facility.

As per the NTP-1999, the Government is committed to provide voice and low speed data services to all the remaining villages by 2002. With the corporatisation of DoT's network by creating BSNL, rural telephony is no more primary responsibility of the public sector. As compared to a self-sustaining expansion of network in the urban areas, service provision in the rural areas is perceived to be unviable. Keeping this in view, policy makers need to focus much more on increasing tele-density in rural areas. The basic draw back in our approach to rural communications so far has been the lack of adequate attempt to built it as a self-sustaining business proposition wherever it is feasible.

There are large sections of the country where the need for subsidy can be eliminated or atleast reduced. This can be done by either utilising commercial activity of a given area (such as areas cultivating cash crops, areas having extensive fisheries or acqua culture, agro-industries etc.) or maximising benefits of convergence, particularly utilising the entertainment segment or E-Government as a killer application. A new policy framework for ensuring the expansion of network at the desired pace and financing it appropriately needs to be put in place at the earliest. USO fund could be one of the major sources of financing this programme. With a view to ensuring efficiency, the provision of telecom services in the rural areas has to be on least-cost basis irrespective of the method of financing these services.

The resources mobilised through the USO Fund mechanism are envisaged to be the prime source of funding the deficit expenditure of providing services in remote, difficult and rural areas. The guidelines for providing financial support under USO have been finalised by the Department of Telecom for implementation of what it calls Universal Service Support Policy (USSP). The support under this policy would be made available from 2002-03. The major highlights of the guidelines issued are :

— The support under the USO fund shall be available to both public access or community telephones and individual household telephones in net high cost rural/remote areas.

— The support from USO Fund shall be provided to meet net cost (i.e. cost - revenue) of providing the universal service.

— Depending upon requirement, the percentage contribution towards Universal Service Levy (USL) could be increased but would be within the prevalent percentage ceiling of licence fee.

— The implementation of the USO will be divided into two clearly identifiable streams i.e. provision of public telecom and information services (Stream - I) and provision of household telephones in high cost rural/ remote areas (Stream - II). Stream-I will be given priority in respect of disbursement of funds.

— Implementation of USO shall be through a multi-layered bidding process on the least quoted subsidy support basis. The lowest bid offering the least subsidy shall be accepted subject to the ceiling of benchmark cost as determined by DOT.

— A separate fund for crediting the receipts towards USO is being set up and will be presently administered by the DoT.

For the present, the rate of USL has been fixed at 5 per cent of the Adjusted Gross Revenue of operators. The detailed terms and conditions applicable to the bidding process are yet to be issued. To ensure complete freedom of functioning, transparency and effectiveness, the administration of the fund need to be entrusted to an autonomous agency under the overall supervision of a Government Department. It is, therefore, proposed that a Universal Services Obligation Board may be created as an autonomous unit under the DoT.

Telecommunications is potentially a profitable sector and service provision by the Government sector i.e. BSNL and MTNL should continue to be financed solely through IEBR. To ensure efficiency of operations and effective competition, the decision-making including investment policies of BSNL and MTNL, need to be purely guided by the commercial considerations. Budget support should be basically restricted to financing the monitoring and regulatory mechanisms only till they become self-financing. But as promoting teledensity in the rural areas is a national objective and if BSNL is asked to shoulder the responsibility of fulfilling Government's commitment in this regard, required budget support may have to be provided for this purpose so as to ensure that it does not go in the red.

The public sector will have to continue to play a significant role in the provision of basic telecom services during the Tenth Plan. Out of about 828 lakh new connections envisaged to be provided during the Tenth Plan, the public sector units i.e. BSNL and MTNL are expected to provide 395.23 lakh additional connections. This assumes no budgetary support from the Government to BSNL for expansion of network in the rural areas. However, depending upon the availability of additional resources through USO support and other sources, public sector may be in a position to achieve much higher targets for major services during the Tenth Plan period. Cellular services are also expected to be the corner-stone of the public sector expansion plans in the Tenth Plan.

As per the plans drawn by the company, BSNL is expected to be a major national player in cellular services. To ensure level playing field to the Public Sector Undertakings, the five year tax holiday under the section 80 I A of Income Tax Act available to private operators needs to be extended to MTNL and BSNL. This may be necessary as a major chunk of the fresh investment envisaged during the Tenth Plan is expected to be made by these two enterprises.

Private investment is also expected to play a leading role in the expansion of telecom services during the Tenth Plan. In the area of value added services, the private sector would continue to play the dominant role. The quantum of investment by the private operators would basically get determined by the rate of return on such investments - both basic as well as value added services. Foreign Direct Investment (FDI) has also a major role to play in supplementing the resources of the domestic private sector as the scale of investment envisaged is large. To boost private sector investment, appropriate policy initiatives need to be undertaken.

The NTP, 1999 has envisaged that India should emerge as a major manufacturing base and major exporter of telecom equipment. The manufacturing capacity of the indigenous industry is small in relation to the other major operators in the world and export constitute a very small proportion of the total production of telecom equipment in the country. Promoting exports as a thrust area and development of Indian multinationals should be among our major goals in this sector. To achieve this objective, the Tenth Plan should aim at removing the various constraints relating to transfer of the latest technology, access to cheap international finance, joint ventures with foreign companies, rationalisation of custom and import duties on inputs and development of a strong industry-sponsored R&D base.

Due to fast changing technology in this sector and the existing technological gap in relation to the developed countries, India will have to rely on transfer of technology in a big way in the immediate future. To achieve this strategic alliance with leading international companies will have to be an integral part of the overall exercise of technology transfer. Strong R&D infrastructure is very vital for promoting a vibrant and strong telecom hardware sector in the country. Telecom R&D also needs to be strengthened in order to have indigenous telecom technology and evolve national standards.

R&D efforts would have to be diversified besides technology development. It should focus on services, systems, processes and markets. This would ensure a user relevant orientation to R&D activities. Applications research also needs to be encouraged so that the research projects become commercially viable and products appropriate for deployment in local conditions are developed. R&D efforts in telecommunications are envisaged to be more effective if these are multi-disciplinary in character. The telecom sector involves some of the most sophisticated concepts in economics, social sciences and management among other disciplines. To give a focused priority attention to R&D activities, some of the specific policy action points are :

— Setting up a Communications Research Council as the apex body to prioritise, plan and finance the R&D projects. It should basically be a industry financed and governed body where the government provides one-time corpus as a grant. The corpus has to be large enough to finance worthy project for 5-6 years to ensure fruitful results.

— The present infrastructure available with Centre for Development of Telematics (C-Dot), the premier body in the Govt. sector, is of such a high standard that it can serve better purpose if it is converted into truly national research organisation. The industry should be fully associated with financing and management of the organisation. It should be able to get worthwhile research projects on its own merits from the proposed Communication Research Council or any other source. Necessary budget support for achieving this transformation may have to be provided till such time C-DoT becomes selffinancing.

— Earmarking a percentage of the turn over of the companies in the organised sector for financing the R&D corpus with a view to ensuring sufficient and regular fund flow to the research activities.

— Giving flexibility to PSU firms to decide adequate perks and pay for retaining the staff engaged in R&D activities as the rate of attrition of human resources due to flight of scientific talent to more attractive outside organisations is very high.

Objectives and Targets of the Tenth Plan

The Tenth plan policies and programmes are guided by the basic goal of creating a worldclass telecom infrastructure in order to meet the requirements of IT based sector and needs of a modernising economy on the least cost basis. Ensuring value for money to the consumers and easy and affordable access to basic telecom services to everyone and everywhere would be the other goal of policies to be pursued in Tenth Plan. The major objectives envisaged for the Tenth Plan are:

(i) Affordable and effective communication facilities to all citizens.

(ii) Provision of universal service to all uncovered areas, including rural areas.

(iii) Building a modern and efficient telecommunications infrastructure to meet the convergence of telecom, IT and the media.

(iv) Transformation of the telecommunications sector to a greater competitive environment providing equal opportunities and level playing field for all the players.

(v) Strengthening R&D efforts in the country.

(vi) Achieving efficiency and transparency in spectrum management

(vii) Protecting the defence and security interests of the country.

(viii) Enabling Indian telecom companies to become truly global players.

The basic thrust of the Tenth Plan would be to provide world level services at affordable prices. With corporatisation of DOT's network, the network expansion/roll-out plans of both Government and private sector would be guided by the demand of various services. In line with the broad objectives of the NTP, 1999 and the objectives envisaged for the Tenth Plan, the following specific targets are envisaged for the telecom sector for the Tenth Plan:

— To endeavour to make available telephones by and large on demand by end of 2002-03 and sustain it thereafter.

— To achieve an overall teledensity of 9.91 by 31st March 2007.

— Achieve telecom coverage of all villages in the country by December 2002 and provide reliable transmission media in all rural areas.

— Provide reliable media to all exchanges by the end of March, 2003.

— Provide high-speed data and multimedia capability using technologies including ISDN to all towns with a population greater than two lakhs by the end of March, 2003.

Expansion of Network During the Tenth Plan

The NTP, 1999 provides the basic framework for the future development and growth of the telecom sector in the country. One of the major objectives of the Policy is to make telephones on demand by the year 2002 and sustain it thereafter so as to achieve a teledensity of 7 by the year 2005 and 15 by the year 2010. Keeping in line with the above goals of teledensity, the country need to achieve an overall teledensity of 9.91 by the Tenth Plan end i.e. March, 2007. To achieve the above target of teledensity, about 650 lakh additional connections may have to be provided during the Tenth Plan.

Working on a different assumption of achieving a tele-density target of 11.5 by March, 2007, the Working Group on Telecom Sector for the Tenth Five Year Plan had recommended that 817.10 lakh new connections needed to be provided during the Tenth Plan. Keeping in view the present trend of growth, the Plans drawn up by the public sector and the availability of funds, the projections of the Working Group seem to be on the higher side. Taking the above factors into account, the goal of achieving teledensity target of 9.91 by March, 2007 seems more realistic.

The distribution among cellular, fixed and WLL based limited mobility lines out of the net addition during the Plan period would depend upon the emerging behaviour of the market, availability of technological innovations and options and relative prices of equipment. As per the initial Plans drawn by Bharat Sanchar Nigam Ltd. (BSNL) and Mahanagar Telephone Nigam Ltd. (MTNL), the public sector is envisaged to provide about 395 lakh additional connections. This implies that remaining connections i.e. about 255 lakh would have to be provided by the private sector of the performance of the private sector is more encouraging higher target of tele density could be achieved.

Bharat Sanchar Nigam Ltd. (BSNL)

Bharat Sanchar Nigam Ltd. (BSNL) came in to existence on 1.10.2000 as a result of the reorganisation of the erstwhile Department of Telecom. With this, the reforms process of separation of policy formulation from service provision and regulation has been completed. This reorganisation had two important implications for BSNL i.e.

(i) BSNL has to act henceforth as a commercial entity; its investment policies among other things to be guided by profits/ purely by commercial consideration.

(ii) BSNL would be subjected to additional financial liabilities like corporate tax, licence fees, payment of dividend etc. which were not applicable to erstwhile DOT.

Besides the above, BSNL has been providing telephones in unremunerative areas including Village Public

Telephones (VPTs) in pursuance of the directives of National Telecom Policy. This obligation is adversely affecting its financial health.

Based on the resources availability of the company, it plans to provide 367.67 lakh new connections during the Tenth Plan. Keeping in line with the projected demand for mobile services, the main focus of the company is envisaged to be on expansion of cellular mobile services as the third operator in various circles. The following table gives the broad details of expansion programme envisaged by the Company during the Tenth Plan:

Table 6. Expansion of Network - BSNL

(In lakh lines)

Type of Phones	Urban	Rural	Total
Fixed	80.00	0.90	80.90
WLL	51.00	11.93	62.93
Mobile	222.00	1.84	223.84
Total	353.00	14.67	367.67

Mahanagar Telephone Nigam Ltd (MTNL)

MTNL had enjoyed monopoly till 2000 in the two metro cities of Delhi and Mumbai, where it operates. Since then the private operators have started providing basic services in Mumbai and are expected to do the same soon in Delhi. Increased competition from private operators is expected during the Tenth Plan. To maintain its position as a major player in Mumbai and Delhi, MTNL envisages to expand its cellular network in a big way during the Tenth Plan.

Expansion of internet services and introduction of IT related services is another major element of company's overall strategy of growth and competition. As per the plans drawn up by the company, 27.56 lakh additional telephone connections are expected to be provided during the Tenth Plan including 11.57 lakh cellular phones. The entire plan outlay of the company is envisaged to be financed out of internal and extra budgetary resources.

ITI Ltd.

ITI Ltd. is the single largest company in the telecom equipment manufacturing sector in the country, both in terms of turnover as well as employment. After suffering losses during 1994-99 period as a result of the policy of global competitive bidding resorted to by DOT and MTNL, the company has staged a turnaround during last two years. It earned a net profit of Rs.27 crore during 2000-01. After disinvestment of HTL Ltd., ITI Ltd. is the only PSU left in the telecom equipment manufacturing sector. The company is also one of the PSUs identified by the Disinvestment Commission for reducing Government's equity to 26 per cent.

The company has developed over the years necessary technological capabilities and have sufficient skilled manpower. The existence of at least one healthy, strong and efficient public sector unit is quite essential to provide the necessary cushion / check against the MNCs. This company can also play and important role in realising our goal of making India a major manufacturing base and exporter of telecom equipment and developing Indian Multinationals in this area.

The company has to be made efficient and competitive to play its due role in the changed scenario. This would call for its strengthening and restructuring, including providing the necessary funds for capital restructuring and allowing them to go in for strategic tie-ups with leading international players. Excess manpower is a major problem with the company. Necessary financial support needs to be arranged to implement an effective Voluntary Retirement Scheme to attain the optimum level of manpower. The company has drawn up further plans for modernisation and diversification in the Tenth Plan. The outlay is envisaged to be financed out of IEBR to be mobilised by the company.

Regulatory Bodies

The Wireless Planning and Coordination (WPC) Wing, set up in 1952, is the national radio regulatory authority to ensure orderly utilisation of radio frequency spectrum and Geo Stationary Orbit (GSO). It is supported by the WMO in this activity. With the opening up of the economy the number of players and services in the telecom sector is bound to increase manifold. Therefore, the Organisation would need to be further strengthened and modernised to enable it to perform its regulatory functions effectively.

The TRAI, set up in 1997, is the apex organisation responsible for performing the regulatory functions in the telecom sector. As a result of the TRAI Amendment Act, 2000, Telecom Dispute and Appellate Tribunal (TDSAT) has been set up. The outlay of these regulatory bodies would continue to be financed out of budget support by the Government till they become self-financing. A World Bank aided project called Telecommunications Sector Reforms Technical Assistance Project is being implemented for modernising and upgrading the facilities in these organisations. The project costing US $ 72 million is envisaged to be implemented over a 4 year period ending December, 2004.

Centre for Development of Telematics (C-DoT)

C-DoT is the main public sector agency engaged in R&D activity in the Telecom sector. It has been a leader in the development of rural exchanges which have performed exceedingly well under tough conditions. C-DoT technology constitutes more than 40per cent of the total lines operative in Indian telecommunications network. C-Dot licence manufacturers are exporting the technology switches to other countries having conditions similar to those in Indian rural areas.

During the Tenth Plan, the thrust of CDoT's research plan would be the development of cost effective technologies providing services and features at par with those being offered by other global players. Development of products to cater to the needs to broad-band fixed and mobile subscribers access system, as well as high band with backbone systems would be an important part of the strategy for the Tenth Plan. Some of the major areas of thrust are:

— Intelligent Network Services

— GSM Personal Communication Services

— Third Generation Mobile Communication System

— Ka Band Satellite Communications

— Cell and Packet Switching Technologies for Voice and Data Convergence

— Ultra High Bit Rate Network Backbone

— Expansion Planning of Existing Wireline Network

Till September, 2000, the plan outlay of CDoT was financed out of I R generated by DoT. With the carving out of BSNL as a separate corporate entity, this mode of financing is no more available and the plan outlay is required to be funded through budgetary support. R&D activity in any sector is very vital for ensuring future growth and hence needs to be supported fully. However it may be mentioned that as one of the major beneficiaries of the R&D of CDoT, the industry needs to be fully associated in financing its activities. Besides, C-DoT needs to focus more on generating internal resources through royalty, consultancy etc. to reduce its dependence on Government support.

Path Ahead

The Tenth Plan would endeavour to build a modern and efficient telecom infrastructure with a view to provide world class telecommunications facilities at affordable rates, meet the needs of convergence of telecom, IT and media and universal service to all uncovered areas. To achieve the above goals, the major initiatives/action points envisaged for the Tenth Plan are :

(i) To achieve a target of tele-density of 9.91 by March, 2007, about 650 lakh new telephone connections need to be provided during the Plan Period.

(ii) The telecom sector needs to be treated as an infrastructure sector for the next decade or so in order to achieve the targets of teledensity in line with the objectives laid out in the NTP, 1999. This is envisaged also to help achieving substantially higher rate of growth of broadband to meet the requirements of other sectors of the economy especially Information Technology and Entertainment.

(iii) Government's broad policy of taxes and regulation for the telecom sector has to be promotional in nature with a view to ensuring optimum growth in the coming years. Revenue generation should not be a major determinant of the macro policy governing the sector. Guided by this principle and keeping in line with the policy adopted by most of the progressive administrations in the world, the licence fee needs to be aligned to the cost of regulation and administration of Universal Service Obligation (USO).

(iv) Ensuring fair and timely interconnection in the multi-operator scenario is one of the major inputs for sustaining high growth. Government's intervention may be required in the form of establishing a fund to finance the requirements of capacity creation especially of incumbent operator to meet increased requirement in this regard.

(v) The policy governing spectrum allocation and licencing has to be so designed that this scarce resource is used optimally and does not become a constraint for growth. Spectrum pricing need to be based on relative demand and supply over space and time in a dynamic manner and should promote introduction of spectrum efficient technology. A significant chunk of available spectrum is being used by defence, police and para military forces. A concrete action plan needs to be put in place to upgrade and modernise the technology being used by these forces so as to ensure efficient and optimal utilisation of spectrum allotted and releasing the surplus spectrum for use by civilian purposes. Necessary funds would have to made available for this purpose.

(vi) The existence of an independent and effective regulatory body is crucial for ensuring optimum growth and free and fair competition. The basic principles that need attention in this regard are:

— Specify time limits for various regulatory procedures.

— Establish a clearly specified schedule of penalties for not meeting the licence conditions and the conditions under which they apply.

— Developing benchmarks for selfregulation by the industry.

— Developing a framework for interaction between regulator and consumer bodies so as to ensure continuous flow of information and feed-back from the consumers in order to achieve desired standards of service quality and regulation.

(vii) Adequacy of funds has to be ensured for effective implementation of the USO. If need arises, the rates of USO levy may have to be increased suitably.

(viii) The policy governing development of rural telecom services need to be promotional in nature with a view to boost teledensity in these areas in line with the objectives of NTP, 1999.

(ix) An outlay of Rs. 86984.00 crore including the budgetary support of Rs. 1500 crore has been approved for the Telecommunications sector for the Tenth Plan.

7

Biotechnlogy Development Strategy

Biotechnology is a knowledge-driven technology, which needs to be driven by a flow of new ideas and concepts in the development of new tools for research, new processes for manufacturing and innovative business models. Rapid responses are needed to meet the challenges as they unfold and there is a requirement for specialized personnel and centres of excellence for R&D. The policy goal for the next decade is to facilitate the availability of scientific and technical human resource in all disciplines relevant to the life science and biotechnology sector.

The recent and continuing advances in life sciences clearly unfold a scenario energized and driven by the new tools of biotechnology. There are a large number of therapeutic biotech drugs and vaccines that are currently being marketed, accounting for a US$40 billion market and benefiting over a hundred million people worldwide. Hundreds more are in clinical development. In addition to these there are a large number of agri-biotech and industrial biotech products that have enormously helped mankind.

The Indian Biotechnology sector is gaining global visibility and is being tracked for emerging investment opportunities. Human capital is perceived to be the key driver for global competitiveness. Added to this is a decreasing appetite for risk capital in developed countries, which has led to a decline in the biotechnology sector in these regions where survival lifelines are being provided by the lower cost research environs of the developing world such as India. For a country like India, biotechnology is a powerful enabling technology that can revolutionize agriculture, healthcare, industrial processing and environmental sustainability.

The Indian biotechnology sector has, over the last two decades, taken shape through a number of scattered and sporadic academic and industrial initiatives. The time is now ripe to integrate these efforts through a pragmatic National Biotechnology Development Strategy. It is imperative that the principal architects of this sector along with other key stakeholders play a concerted role in formulating such a strategy to ensure that we not only build on the existing platform but expand the base to create global leadership in biotechnology by unleashing the full potential of all that India has to offer.

Biotechnology is Important to India

Biotechnology can deliver the next wave of technological change that can be as radical and even more pervasive than that brought about by IT. Employment generation, intellectual wealth creation, expanding entrepreneurial opportunities, augmenting industrial growth are a few of the compelling factors that warrant a focused approach for this sector. Biotechnology as a business segment for India has the potential of generating revenues to the tune of US$ 5 Billion and creating one million jobs by 2010 through products and services. This can propel India into a significant position in the global biotech sweepstakes.

Biopharmaceuticals alone have the potential to be a US$ 2 billion market opportunity largely driven by vaccines and biogenerics.Clinical development services can generate in excess of US$1.5 billion whilst bioservices or outsourced research services can garner a market of US$1 billion over this time scale. The balance US$500 million is attributable to agricultural and industrial biotechnology. India has many assets in its strong pool of scientist and engineers, vast institutional network and cost effective manufacturing. There are over a hundred National Research Laboratories employing thousands of scientists.

There are more than 300 college level educational and training institutes across the country offering degrees and diplomas in biotechnology, bio-informatics and the biological sciences, producing nearly 500,000 students on an annual basis. More than 100 medical colleges add ~17,000 medical practitioners per year. About 300,000 postgraduates and 1500 PhDs qualify in biosciences and engineering each year. These resources need to be effectively marshaled, championed and synergized to create a productive enterprise. India is reorganized as a mega bio-diversity country and biotechnology offers opportunities to convert our biological resources into economic wealth and employment opportunities. Innovative products and services that draw on renewable resources bring greater efficiency into industrial processes, check environmental degradation and deliver a more bio-based economy.

Indian agriculture faces the formidable challenge of having to produce more farm commodities for our growing human and livestock population from diminishing per capita arable land and water resources. Biotechnology has the potential to overcome this challenge to ensure the livelihood security of 110 million farming families in our country. The advancement of biotech as a successful industry confronts many challenges related to research and development, creation of investment capital, technology transfer and technology absorption, patentability and intellectual property, affordability in pricing, regulatory issues and public confidence. Central to this are two key factors: affordability and accessibility to the products of biotechnology.

Policies that foster a balance between sustaining innovation and facilitating technology diffusion need to be put in place. There are several social concerns that need to be addressed in order to propel the emergence of biotechnology innovation in our country such as conserving bioresources and ensuring safety of products and processes. Government and industry have to play a dual role to advance the benefits of modern biotechnology while at the same time educate and protect the interests of the public. Wide utilization of new technologies would require clear demonstration of the new added value to all stakeholders.

The National Science and Technology Policy of the Government and the Vision Statement on Biotechnology issued by the Department of Biotechnology have directed notable interventions in the public and private sectors to foster life sciences and biotechnology. There has been substantial progress in terms of support for R&D, human resource generation and infrastructure development over the past decade. With the introduction of the product patent regime it is imperative to achieve higher levels of innovation in order to be globally competitive. The challenge now is to join the global biotech league. This will require larger investments and an effective functioning of the innovation pathway.

Capturing new opportunities and the potential economic, environmental, health and social benefits will challenge government policy, public awareness, educational, scientific, technological, legal and institutional framework. The issue of access to the products arising from biotechnology research in both medicine and agriculture is of paramount importance. Therefore, there should be adequate support for public good research designed to reach the unreached in terms of technology empowerment. Both "public good" and "for profit" research should become mutually reinforcing. Public institutions and industry both have an important role in the process.

The National Biotechnology Development Strategy takes stock of what has been accomplished and provides a framework for the future within which strategies and specific actions to promote biotechnology can be taken. The policy framework is a result of wide consultation with stakeholders - scientists, educationists, regulators, representatives of society and others and reflects their consensus. It focuses on cross-cutting issues such as human resource development academic and industry interface, infrastructure development, lab and manufacturing, promotion of industry and trade, biotechnology parks and incubators, regulatory mechanisms, public education and awareness building.

This policy also aims to chalk out the path of progress in sectors such as agriculture and food biotechnology, industrial biotechnology, therapeutic and medical biotechnology, regenerative and genomic medicine, diagnostic biotechnology, bio-engineering, nano-biotechnology, bio-informatics and IT enabled biotechnology, clinical biotechnology, manufacturing & bio-processing, research services, bio-resources, environment and intellectual property & patent law. Several state governments have enunciated biotech policies spelling out a comprehensive blueprint for the sector. It is, therefore, prudent to have a National Biotech Development Strategy that charts an integrated 10-year road map with clear directions and destinations.

This is the time for investment in frontier technologies such as biotechnology. It is envisaged that clearly thought-out strategies will provide direction and enable action by various stakeholders to achieve the full potential of this exciting field for the social and economic well being of the nation.

Policy Recommendations and Interventiions

Biotechnology, globally recognized as a rapidly emerging and far-reaching technology, is aptly described as the "technology of hope" for its promising of food, health and environmental sustainability. In order to build a successful biotechnology sector, large talent pools are required in multiple scientific disciplines such as molecular and cell biology, chemistry, physics, engineering, bioinformatics, medicine, agriculture, microbiology, technology transfer & commercialization, bioentreprise & biofinancing and intellectual property rights management.

Product and process development are interdisciplinary in nature and deficiencies in specific areas may weaken the whole sector. The key issue is the manner in which to create an effective interface across disciplines. Reliable estimates of human resource availability for the next 10 years are required. Expert consensus indicates that there is adequate enrollment currently at the post-graduate and under-graduate levels, however the quality is inconsistent. Areas such as intellectual property rights, regulatory issues and industrial training have received inadequate attention. There is a consensus that there is an urgent need to augment the number of Ph.D. programs in the Life Sciences and biotechnology. A strong pool of academic leaders is key to sustained innovation. Strategic Actions are given below:

National Task Force on education & training:

— A National Task Force will be created to formulate model undergraduate and postgraduate curricula in Life Sciences keeping in view, future needs. The said curricula must address the underlying need for multidisciplinary and inter-disciplinary learning and the appropriate stage for biotechnology training.

Need assessment

— There would be need assessment in 2005 for the next five years and close monitoring during the period for interim changes.

— A 10-year perspective plan for human resource will be prepared every five years.

Curriculum development

— Course curricula will be reviewed and improved in consultation with industry and research establishments and standard e-learning modules will be developed for specific skill areas such as IPR, regulations, and bioentreprise.

— Hands on exposure to M.Sc. biotechnology students will be enhanced through an extended industry internship as well as through short-term placements at CSIR and other appropriate National Institutes.

— Dual degree programs in biotechnology that include regulatory matters, IPR and bio-enterprise management will be encouraged and supported by the Department of Biotechnology.

— Emphasis will be given on training of high quality technicians and technologists in skills required by the industry by establishing Regional training centres at diploma, graduate and postgraduate levels.

Quality improvement

— An accreditation mechanism will be put in place for ensuring minimum standard of education and training at the post graduate and undergraduate levels. Base requirements for teaching and laboratory infrastructure will be specified and enforced.

— Teachers training programs will be taken up by creating regional teachers training centres

Strengthening of teaching and R&D in life sciences and biotechnology in the university system

— Strengthening R&D in Life sciences and biotechnology in the university system will be accorded high priority. This is considered important for improving the quality of education and providing exposure to new technologies for students at various levels. Specific mechanisms to achieve the goal will include

— Creation of inter-disciplinary centres of excellence with world class infrastructure in key areas

— Program support to encourage inter-departmental networking

— Visiting professorship and creation of industry sponsored chairs in partnership with the Department of Biotechnology.

Attracting talent to life science and biotechnology

— Bright students will be attracted to take up careers in biology and biotechnology through special scholarships. Summer assignments at Academic and Industry research laboratories will be introduced at the school level to create interest in the fields of biotechnology and biology

— Women scientists will be encouraged to take up careers in biotechnology. Service conditions will be liberalized for women to be able to return to research/academics after maternity breaks.

Creating science & technology leaders for the industry

— The number of Ph.D fellowships offered by the Department of Biotechnology will be increased to 200 per annum

— Public-private partnerships will be encouraged in Ph.D programs through creation of the 'Bio-edu-Grid'- a network of universities and industries facilitating pooling of resources.

— Masters degree level professionals in industry will be encouraged to undertake Ph.D. programs while retaining their jobs through industryuniversity tie-ups.

Arresting and reversing brain drain

— As mentioned earlier, the number of postdoctoral fellowships offered by the Department of Biotechnology will be increased to 200 per annum in order to attract talent.

— Outstanding young investigator grants in biotechnology will be introduced. This will provide a package including salary support, research grant, equipment and opportunities to attend national and international conferences. The salary support under the scheme will be at par with that of entry-level faculty positions.

— Information on availability of positions in education/research establishments and industries will be provided on a website to facilitate employment of scientists with specific skills at appropriate positions.

— A database of scientists working in different areas of biotechnology within and outside the country will be created to utilize the expertise appropriately.

Enabling working conditions for scientists to undertake industry oriented research

— Lateral mobility of scientific personnel: Scientists working at universities and research institutions may be allowed to work in industries for commercialization of their research efforts. This could be in the form of secondment or consultancy with industry or by a sabbatical for three years during the working life of scientists

— Dual/adjunct faculty positions: Researchers working in university/research institutions may be allowed to hold positions in the industry and vice-versa

— Joint salary support: Faculty employed in academic institutions may be allowed to hold positions for a period of time in which their salary is contributed both by the industry and the academic institution on a mutually agreed basis.

— Rapid travel grants: Rapid travel grants scheme for approval within two weeks for young scientists to interact with mentors and industry collaborators would be initiated.

— Institute Innovation grants through the Department of Biotechnology to fund academic researchers to develop their concepts into patentable and more importantly licensable technologies. Such grants may be utilized for the purpose of providing additional infrastructure and manpower, patenting costs as well as costs related to proof of concept studies.

These steps will ensure that the large available resources of human talent in biotechnology are supported and this will guarantee the progress of the biotech sector.

Infrastructure Development and Manufacturing

The strength of a biotechnology company lies in up

scaling a number of proven technologies - diagnostics, vaccines, products, and processes - for fine-tuning and large-scale production. While Indian industry is strong in product development and marketing for commercial benefits, biotechnology in India still lacks the infrastructure required to take up R&D in areas like molecular modeling, protein engineering, drug designing, immunological studies, preclinical studies, clinical trials, etc. In order to get the best from public and privately funded biological/biotechnological research, it is imperative to utilize the infrastructure generated optimally for societal benefits.

The concept of contract research organizations (CROs), contract manufacturing organizations (CMOs), contract packagers, lab services providers etc., is steadily taking shape in India. In the area of biomanufacturing, industry estimates that the market for biogenerics in India is expected to see a 43 percent jump from Rs 308.50 crore in 2001 to Rs 1,305.7 crore in 2005 and projected to reach Rs 1,864.3 crore by 2007 registering a growth of 19 percent.

India's strengths lie in the availability of educated and skilled manpower, proficiency in English, low capital and operational costs and the proven track record in meeting international standards of quality. There is ample proof that the Indian companies are committed to global standards. According to reports, outside of the US, India ranks the highest with 61 USFDA-approved plants and in excess of 200 GMP certified pharmaceutical manufacturing facilities.

Strategic Actions:

— Department of Biotechnology will act to facilitate a Single Window Clearance mechanism for establishing Biotechnology plants.

— Encourage private participation in infrastructure development like roads, water supply and effluent treatment.

— Depositories of biological materials will be created in partnership with industry on IDA model for agriculturally important organisms, medically important organisms, plasmids, cosmids and constructs of special nature generated with adequate human interventions

— State of the art large animal house facilities with GLP will be created for testing candidate vaccines and biotherapeutics. Testing facilities will be created for GMO/LMO

Promotion of Industry and Trade

The emergence of India as a global player in the biotech sector requires government to play the role of a champion and foster an international competitive environment for investment and enterprise development. India's strategy must be to get more value from its R&D investment and from IPR generation. The Biotechnology sector has in recent years witnessed accelerated growth. With approximately 200 industries the growth of the biotech sector in India has been rapid.

Current estimates indicate that the industry grew by 39% annually to reach a value of US$ 705 million in 2003-2004. Total investment also increased in 2003-2004 by 26% to reach US$ 137 million. Exports presently account for 56% of revenue. Currently the biopharma sector occupies the largest market share of 76% followed by bio-agri 8.42%, bioservices 7.70%, industrial products 5.50% and bioinformatics 2.45%. The bioservice sector registered the highest growth (100%) in 2003-2004 with bioagri 63.64% and biopharma 38.55%. The current policy review envisages an annual turnover of US$ 5 billion by 2010.

India has to develop its own biotechnological and pharmaceutical products to ensure quality and affordability for global trade.

In addition to opportunities in drug discovery and development there are significant openings to provide services to the worldwide biotech and pharmaceutical industries and to leverage low cost high quality manufacturing with a global discovery potential. Capitalizing on these opportunities would create many new valuable jobs in India as we have seen in the outsourcing and service industry. However, to achieve the targeted business volume, several new challenges have to be met. These are predictable and enabling policies, increased public and private support for early or proof-of-concept stage of product development; improved communication among stakeholders in the sector, public-private partnerships, integration of the Indian biotech sector globally; and improved infrastructure. The vision is to maximize opportunities in the area of contract research, manufacturing and to promote discovery and innovation.

The Biotech industry being capital intensive in nature has historically relied on venture capital from public and private sources. India needs to provide active support through incubator funds, seed funds and provision of various incentives in order to develop the biotech sector. In a highly competitive and fast moving business environment, innovative capacity is an important determinant of the ability to create a continuing pipeline of new products and processes. Innovation covers knowledge creation (R&D), knowledge diffusion (education and training) and knowledge application (commercialization).

Innovation is not a one-time event; instead, it has to continuously respond to changing circumstances for creating sustainable growth. Innovation is measured in terms of external / domestic patent applications; human capital devoted to R&D, government expenditure on R&D proportionate to country's GDP, business funded expenditure on R&D, indigenous technologies standardized, demonstrated and transferred to industry for commercialization; and the number of spin off companies created. Clear government policies for promotion of innovation and commercialization of knowledge will propel the growth of the biotechnology sector. Strategic Actions are given below:

Innovation:

— Basic and translational research in key biological processes and new materials will be supported as innovation for tomorrow. Access to the knowledge generated will be improved by supporting knowledge and social networks among stakeholders so that those with appropriate skills can convert the research output into useful products and processes.

— Research to promote innovation must be supported increasingly on a cooperative rather than a competitive basis. This requires effective communication among science agencies, research institutions, academia and industry.

— To promote India as a hub of innovation, a network of relevant stakeholders should be developed. Public investment should be used as a catalyst to promote such clustering and networking as this can lead to enhanced creativity by sharing of expertise, resources and infrastructure.

— Availability of human resource would be ensured at each phase of the product cycle.

— Strengthening technology transfer capacity

It is proposed to create several national/regional technology transfer cells (TTC's) over the next 5 years to provide high caliber, specialized and comprehensive technology transfer services. The services would include: evaluating technology and identifying potential commercial uses, developing and executing and intellectual property protection strategies identifying potential licensees and negotiating licenses. Each TTC would service a cluster of institutions in a region or a large city. Optimal delivery of services by the TTCs requires professionals with background in industry and science, wide networks, an external focus and high level licensing skills.

The best practices for effective technology transfer will be benchmarked. The skills of existing technology transfer professionals will be upgraded by a combination of specialized training courses, including linking to important programs redesigning the incentives and career paths for posting. Scientists and other innovators shall be equipped with a better understanding of markets and commercialization pathways, the process of technology transfer, the strategy of protecting intellectual property rights and industrial licensing.

Fiscal and trade policy initiatives: Biotechnology firms are by far the most research intensive among major industries. On an average the biotechnology sector invests 20-30 % of its operating costs in R&D or technology outsourcing. Government support, fiscal incentives and tax benefits are therefore critical to this sector. These measures will also help to capitalize on the inherent cost effectiveness of the Indian biotech enterprise. The suggested interventions include:

— Exemption of import duties on key R&D, contract manufacturing / clinical trial equipment and duty credit for R&D consumer goods to enable small and medium entrepreneurs to reduce the high capital cost of conducting research.

— Extending the 150 % weighted average tax deduction on R&D expenditure under section 35 (2AB) until 2010 and to permit international patenting costs under this provision and enable eligibility of expenditure incurred with regard to filing patents outside India for weighted deductions u/s 35 (2 ab)

— Enable lending by banks to biotech companies as priority sector lending. Currently banks are almost averse to lending to young biotech companies. In order to encourage banks to lend and provide banking services to the biotech sector, a significant push through appropriate policy guidelines from the Reserve Bank of India is necessary. Currently lending to agri-businesses as well as investment in Venture Funds by banks is categorized as Priority Sector Lending. Biotech as a business has similar characteristics in terms of risk as well as gestation time lines and it is therefore recommended that lending to Biotech be also categorized as Priority Sector lending.

— Remove customs duty on raw materials imported into India, where the finished product is imported duty free. Life Saving Drugs imported and sold in India are exempted from paying customs duty; whereas raw materials for diagnostics and other pharmaceutical biotech products manufactured in India are levied customs duty. To promote the indigenous manufacturing industry and make it competitive globally, raw materials imported by Indian manufacturers should be eligible for Duty Drawback.

— Rationalization of import and export of biological material is considered critical for clinical research and business process outsourcing.

— Simplification and streamlining of procedures for import, clearance and storage of biologicals, land acquisition, obtaining environmental and pollution control approvals would be simplified and streamlined within shorter time frame lines through consultations with various central and state government departments.

— As an effective regulatory mechanism has been put in place though recent interventions, Foreign Investment Promotion Board (FIPB) approval for equity investment may no longer be necessary.

— Joint R&D collaboration and generation of joint IP though global partnerships would be fostered.

— International trade opportunities would be promoted to guide R&D investment Indian biotech strengths would be aggressive by promoted globally.

— Efforts would be made to remove hurdles for contract research especially for input output norms and tax on revenue generated through contract research / R&D.

— Easy access to information, regarding legislation and rules and regulations for transboundary movements of biologicals would be promoted.

— Current standards and safety of products would be enhanced.

— Efforts would be strengthened to promote acceptance of Indian regulatory data internationally.

— Research, trade and industrial partnership would be fostered at regional and sub-regional levels.

— A "cluster" approach would be encouraged to operations. One significant features of the industry is the fluidity and variety of its intercompany relationships, traditionally much greater than in other industries. It has relied to a considerable degree on contracting and outsourcing, especially "upstream" in R&D through various licensing arrangements and "downstream" through co-marketing agreements.

— Collaborative knowledge networks would be promoted. Expanded sharing of information, including creation/use of collaborative knowledge networks (CKN), can greatly enhance a company's performance under a cluster approach. Managing the many external relationships is complex. Flexible and pervasive communications systems that allow information to flow effortlessly within and between contracting organizations will provide the key to success. Increasingly, IT advances, including webbased approaches, will provide the foundation for these systems.

Public investment for promotion of innovation and knowledge commercialization: Availability of financial support for early phase of product development to establish proof-of-principle is the key to sustaining innovation. In this context, it is proposed to institute 'Small Business Innovation Research Initiative' (SBIRI) scheme through the Department of Biotechnology in 2005-06 for supporting small and medium size enterprises as a grant/loan. Companies with up to 1000 employees will be eligible. The scheme will support pre-proof of concept, early stage innovative research and provide mentorship and problem solving support in addition to the grant / soft loan. The SBIRI scheme will operate in two phases of innovation and product development.

SBIRI Phase - I : The funding in this stage will be provided for highly innovative, early stage, pre-proof-of-concept research. Preference will be given to proposals that address important national needs. The maximum amount of funding to an enterprise will be limited to Rs. 50 lakh with not more than 50% of it going as grant and the remaining as an interest free loan. For projects to be considered at this stage, though a partner from a public R&D institution would be considered important, it will not be a mandatory requirement for those companies that have good quality scientists. This should encourage high quality scientists to agree to work in small and medium biotech companies, a change from our traditions. The R & D requirement of the public institution will be met through a grant.

SBIRI Phase - II : It is expected that some of the proposals funded with SBIRI Phase-I will establish the proof-of-concept. At this stage, the ability of the project to get venture capital funding improves. Such projects will be eligible for Phase-II funding. Some projects could be eligible for direct phase-II support. It is proposed to provide soft loan at this stage for product development nd commercialization at an interest rate of 2%. The role of public R&D institution at this stage too is critical. The partner in the public institution at this stage will get the R&D support as grant.

Small and medium knowledge-based industries in biotech sector will be encouraged to avail of equity support from the SME Growth Fund of Small Industries Development Bank of India (SIDBI).

Code of best practice for disclosure guidelines: Setting up a 'Code for Best Practice for Disclosure Guidelines for the Indian Biotech Industry'. This Code will be a part of the General Listing Requirements and Disclosure Guidelines and will be in conjunction with SEBI's General Listing Rules and Disclosure Guidelines.

Establishing Biotechnology Parks

Establishing biotechnology parks for the growth of the biotechnology industry is essential either through public-private alliance or public/private sponsorships. With its large human resource in molecular biology, microbiology, biochemical engineering, synthetic organic chemistry, chemical engineering and allied branches of engineering and strong institutional base at the universities, CSIR,

ICMR and ICAR, India is well placed to support a number of biotech parks. Biotechnology Parks can provide a viable mechanism for licensing new technologies to upcoming biotech companies to start new ventures and to achieve early stage value enhancement of the technology with minimum financial inputs. These biotech parks facilitate the lab to land transfer of the technologies by serving as an impetus for entrepreneurship through partnership among innovators from universities, R&D institutions and industry.

Basic minimum components for parks should include research laboratories for product development, multi-purpose pilot facility for manufacturing and process development, quality control and validation of technologies, common effluent treatment plant, a GLP Animal House, a recognized human resource training centre, administrative support centre etc. The biotech parks should be located so as to be easily accessible for all the stakeholders, tenants, academia with connecting roads, water and power supply and should also attract less administrative clearances from the government.

Strategic Actions are as follows:

— The Department of Biotechnology will promote and support at least 10 biotech parks by 2010. Each park will necessarily meet the qualifying criteria related to the characteristics of the location, a viable business plan, management strategy and a clear definition of the partners and their roles.

— The Department of Biotechnology will support creation of incubators in biotech parks promoted by a private industry or through public-private partnership in the form of grant upto 30% of the total cost or upto 49% in the form of equity.

— It is proposed that a central body Biotechnology Parks Society of India (BPSI) be set up for the promotion of biotechnology parks in the country on the same lines of the Software technology Parks of India (STPI). The BPSI should be run by professionals having experience in the areas of biotechnology, knowledge in Acts and Rules relevant to biotechnology and management skills. The existing parks can become members of these new biotech parks.

The BPSI would be responsible for evaluating the project proposals and advising the Department of Biotechnology on the funding pattern; facilitating industries in obtaining industrial, environmental and other relevant approvals from the central government; making recommendation regarding fiscal incentives to be granted to the biotechnology parks; providing guidance to the venture capital institutions on investment in biotech parks; providing accreditation to the parks etc.

— Concessions to biotech companies located in biotech parks Biotech companies located at biotech parks are eligible for benefits as per the recent changes in the Foreign Trade Policy:

— Duty free import of equipment, instruments and consumables.

— Tax holiday under Section 10A/ 10B of the Income Tax Act

— A scheme will be put in place for operationalising of the incentives to biotech units located in biotech parks. As a part of this scheme biotech company located in biotech parks to be allowed a five-year time frame to meet the export obligation norms under the SEZ scheme. This measure helps to address the long and unpredictable gestational time lines that are inherent to biotech product development.

Regulatory Mechanisms

It is important that biotechnology is used for the social benefit of India and for economic development. To fulfill this vision, it has to be ensured that research and application in biotechnology is guided by a process of decision-making that safeguards both human health and the environment with adherence to the highest ethical standards.

There is consensus that existing legislation, backed by science based assessment procedures clearly articulates rules and regulations that can efficiently fulfill this vision. Choices are required to be made that reflect an adequate balance between benefit, safety, access and the interest of consumers and farmers. It is also important that biotechnology products that are required for social and economic good are produced speedily and at the lowest cost. A scientific, rigorous, transparent, efficient, predictable, and consistent regulatory mechanism for biosafety evaluation and release system/ protocol is an essential for achieving these multiple goals.

Strategic Actions are as follows:

— The recommendation of the Swaminathan Committee on regulation of agri-biotech products and of the Mashelkar committee on recombinant pharma products will be implemented in 2005

— It is recommended that an event that has already undergone extensive biosafety tests should not be treated as a new event if it is in a changed background containing the tested and biosafety evaluated "event". Where adequate evidence is available that the recurrent parent genetic background of a notified/registered genotype is nearly restored (through field data/ molecular data), only the agronomic performance and the level and stability of the transgene expression may be analyzed by two-year trial data by the ICAR.

Even in case of a structurally altered transgene with no significant modifications in protein conformation, the toxicity and allergenicity tests need not be carried out provided the predicted antigenic epitope remains the same and the level of expression of the transgene is within the defined limits. For the released event, Department is of the view that there is no need of large-scale trials under the Genetic Engineering Approval Committee, as the biosafety aspects have been already addressed adequately before releasing the "event". Only ICAR trials may address the agronomic evaluation of the crop.

— An inter-ministerial group chaired by a reputed scientist will be established in 2005 to address anomalies and issues that arise in regulation from time to time. It is proposed that the administrative support to this committee be through the Department of Biotechnology.

The mandate of the committee should be to vet any changes in policies, procedures, protocols by departments dealing with regulation in biotech products and processes; resolve issues emanating from the overlapping/conflicting rules in various acts related to regulation of biotechnology activities in R&D, import, export, releases etc. and to review guidelines, protocols, standard operating procedures and ensure their dissemination to all stakeholders from time to time

— A competent single National Biotechnology Regulatory Authority be established with separate divisions for agriculture products/transgenic crops, pharmaceuticals/drugs and industrial products; and transgenic food/feed and transgenic animal/aqua culture. The authority is to be governed by an independent administrative structure with common chairman. The inter-ministerial group will evolve suitable proposals for consideration of the government.

— A centre for in-service training of all professionals, irrespective of their location, engaged in the regulatory process to be established by the Department of Biotechnology in close collaboration with other concerned departments and institutions.

— All existing guidelines to be updated and made consistent with the recommendations of the Swaminathan and Mashelkar committees in 2005. New guidelines on transgenic research and product/process development in animal, aqua culture, food, phyto-pharma and environmental application to be put in place in 2005 by the concerned ministries/departments

— As an interim measure, a special regulatory cell will be created by the DBT to build capacity in the country for scientific risk assessment, monitoring and management, to foster international linkages, support biosafety research; to obtain and review feedback from different stakeholders and provide support to industry and R&D institutions. This cell will only have a promotional and catalytic role

— Measures will be taken to build professionalism and competence in all agencies involved with regulation of biotechnology products

— Research is support of regulation, to safeguard health and environment shall be supported by the concerned funding agencies to generate knowledge that will guide regulations and bioethics policy.

— Concerned ministries will make a vigorous effort to promote acceptance of the Indian regulatory decisions by other trading countries.

Public Communication and Participation

Biotechnology today has become as important as traditional plant and animal breeding have been in the past. At the same time, it raises a number of difficult economic, social, ethical, environmental and political issues that constitute major challenges for the human society. The reception of biotech products by the public has been rather mixed. In general biopharmaceutical products seem to be better accepted than transgenic crops. Clearly it is no longer possible to assume automatic public acceptance of new products and processes that promise public and commercial benefits.

Public perception and opinion have a significant influence on the direction and funding of biotechnology research. Hence there is a need to work actively and transparently to inform and engage the civic society in decision-making, and to maintain a relationship of trust and confidence. The government and the industry must actively promote access to information on the benefits and risks in a balanced manner. To achieve this goal, several enabling factors already exist: a sound biosafety regulatory system; well respected appellate and judicial system for redressal of grievances; cadre of willing and able scientists for effective and accurate communication of information; a large body of extension personnel in agriculture, fisheries, veterinary and human health sectors; large NGO network spread across the country; and an effective and independent mass media.

However, several challenges to success need to be recognized while framing the strategies: diverse levels of education and literacy across the country; low understanding of biotechnology among the public; lack of simple communication material; varying quality of science reporting; inadequate inter agency coordination; insufficient dialogue between scientists, industry, policy makers, regulators, consumer for a civil society organizations and the mass media; and lack of sufficiently proactive administrative machinery.

There is a need to build public awareness about opportunities and challenges presented by biotechnology development and to inspire public trust and confidence on the safety, efficacy as well as social and ethical acceptability of products among consumers and civil society through the dissemination of accurate information in a coherent, balanced well articulated, user-friendly and transparent manner. Several focused and well-directed measures are needed to achieve public trust and confidence in biotechnology. Strategic Actions are as follows:

Create a cadre of resource persons to reach the stakeholders

— Creation of a cadre of resource persons to provide credible information based on scientific data

— Training media personnel through Institutes of Mass Communication, colleges of journalism and others

— Capacity building among extension personnel in agricultural, fisheries, veterinary and medical sectors

— Involvement of Panchayati Raj institutions in the process of analysis and understanding the risks and benefits associated with GMOs as they will be playing an important role in the local level management of biodiversity, access to benefit sharing etc.

— Awareness generation among undergraduate and post-graduate students in universities, colleges etc on issues related to biosafety.

— Promoting a genetic literacy movement within government and public schools through 50 genome clubs nature clubs each year.

Creating a media resource network

— To facilitate access to information

Empowering policy makers

— Regular training programs for policy makers

Empowering the judiciary

— Setting up a training school for the judiciary under the aegis of Centre for DNA Fingerprinting and Diagnostics, Hyderabad

— Training through the National Law Schools and other similar institutions

Institutional mechanisms for strengthening public trust

— Establishment of a dedicated training centre for biosafety, food and nutrition safety and standards as per codex alimentarius committee.

— Creation of a 'National Biotechnology Awareness Fund' for providing support for the education and preparation of educational resource material for various sections of stakeholders in different regional languages of the country

Agriculture and Food Biotechnology

Biotechnology is necessary to maintain our agriculture competitive andremunerative and to achieve nutrition security in the face of major challenges such as declining per capita availability of arable land; lower productivity of crops, livestock and fisheries, heavy production losses due to biotic (insects pests, weeds) and abiotic (salinity, drought, alkalinity) stresses; heavy postharvest crop damage and declining availability of water as an agricultural input. Investment in agricultural related biotechnology has resulted in significantly enhanced R&D capability and institutional building over the years.

However, progress has been rather slow in converting the research leads into usable products.

Uncertainties regarding IPR management and regulatory requirements, poor understanding of risk assessment and lack of effective management and commercialization strategies have been significant impediments. India owns very few genes of applied value. The majority of the genes under use - about 40 - are currently held by MNCs and have been received under material transfer agreements for R&D purpose without clarity on the potential for commercialization.

The spectrum of biotechnology application in agriculture is very wide and includes generation of improved crops, animals, plants of agro forestry importance; microbes; use of molecular markers to tag genes of interest; accelerating of breeding through marker - assisted selection; fingerprinting of cultivars, land raises, germplasm stocks; DNA based diagnostics for pests / pathogens of crops, farm animals and fish; assessment and monitoring of bio diversity; in vitro mass multiplication of elite planting material; embryo transfer technology for animal breeding; food and feed biotechnology. Plants and animals are being used for the production of therapeutically or industrially useful products, the emphasis being on improving efficiency and lowering the cost of production.

However, emphasis should not be on edible vaccines for which use in real life condition is difficult. Nutrition and balanced diet are emerging to be important health promotional strategies. Biotechnology has a critical role in developing and processing value added products of enhanced nutritive quality and providing tools for ensuring and monitoring food quality and safety. It has been estimated that if Biofertilizers were used to substitute only 25% of chemical fertilizers on just 50% of India's crops the potential would be 2,35,000 MT. Today about 13,000 MT of Biofertilizers are used - only 0.36% of the total fertilizer use.

The projected production target by 2011 is roughly around 50,000 MT. Biopesticides have fared slightly better with 2.5% share of the total pesticide market of 2700 crores and an annual growth rate of 10-15 %. In spite of the obvious advantages, several constraints have limited their wider usage such as products of inconsistent quality, short shelf life, sensitivity to drought, temperature, and agronomic conditions. From a research perspective the spectrum of organisms studied has been rather narrow and testing has been on limited scale and restricted mainly to agronomic parameters.

Environmental factors such as survival in the Rhizosphere / phyllosphere and competition of native microbes have not received sufficient attention. Moreover, results on crops are slow to show. Unless there is a policy initiative at the centre and the state to actively promote Biofertilizers and biopesticides at a faster pace, there is unlikely to be a quantum jump in their consumption. A taskforce headed by Dr MS Swaminthan (2004) under the Ministry of Agriculture has prepared a detailed framework on the application of biotechnology in agriculture. The report rightly lays emphasis on the judicious use of biotechnologies for the economic well being of farm families, food security of the nation, health security of the consumer, protection of the environment, and security of national and international trade in farm commodities.

Principles

Consistent with the overall vision outlined by MS Swaminathan taskforce, the priorities in agri-biotech would be based on social, economic, ecological, ethical, and gender equity issues. The following guiding principles would apply across the sector:

— A comprehensive and integrated view should be developed of r-DNA and non r-DNA based applications of biotechnology with other technological components required for agriculture as a whole

— Use of conventional biotechnologies (e.g. biofertilizers, biopesticides, bioremediation technologies, molecular assisted grading, plant tissue culture etc.) should continue to be encouraged and supported. A precautionary, yet promotional approach should be adopted in employing transgenic R&D activities based on technological feasibility, socio-economic considerations and promotion of trade.

— Public funding should be avoided to research areas of low priority or those that could reduce employment and impinge the livelihood of rural families.

— Regulatory requirement in compliance with Cartagena Protocol, another international treaty and protocol for biosafety, germplasm exchange and access and the guiding principles of codex alimentarius will be implemented through inter ministerial consultative process

— Transgenic plants should not be commercialized in crops/commodities where our international trade may be affected. However, their use may be allowed for generation of proof of principle, strictly for R&D, their alternate systems are not available or not suitable.

— In a long term perspective basic research for development of low volume, high value secondary and tertiary products through enabling technologies of genomics, proteomics, engineering of metabolic pathways, RNAi, host pathogen interaction and others. Research and support of biosafety regulation would need support. It is proposed to do away with the large-scale field-testing of the released transgenic events and make it compliant to agronomic test requirements.

Strategic Actions are as follows:

Accelerating the pace of product development

— In our quest for better products, strong and sustained support should be given to encourage indigenous discovery of new genes and promoters in both public and privately owned institutions. Nevertheless, wherever there be an urgent need for a product to achieve food or nutritional security, creative commercial and academic international partnerships should be explored in national interest for sourcing important genes and promoters through licensing arrangements on exclusive/non-exclusive basis. The cost effectiveness should be carefully assessed on a case-to-case basis.

— A gene bank should be created and be accessible to private and public sector organizations after payment of an appropriate fee.

Public-Private Partnership

— There is an urgent need to promote and improve the levels of horizontal integration between public-public and public-private laboratories.

— Institutions that generate knowledge and those that specialize in late stage field trials are currently compartmentalized. While support to public-funded innovation must continue to be strengthened, it is proposed that at least 30% of government-funded programmes must have a commercial partner who will be responsible for directing R&D towards commercialization. Public investment should also be encouraged in small and medium companies, especially for late stage trials of transgenic crops.

Partnership between public-funded organizations and industry is crucial in the science-to-product chain.

Inter-ministerial Agriculture Biotechnology Board: An inter-ministerial Agriculture Biotechnology Board involving Ministry of Agriculture, ICAR, DBT, MoEF, regulatory authority, expert scientists, industry, and the farming community should be established to continuously assess cross cutting issues such as: duplication of R&D investments; capacity building; promotion of horizontal partnerships between various components in the knowledge-product chain; the most cost-effective manner of overcoming nutrition deficiencies (viz. iron, zinc, iodine, vitamin A); availability, access, release and efficient system for biosafety assessment of GMOs and products thereof; safe use of approved technologies and prevention of unauthorized ones; building public trust and understanding biotechnological application relating to global warming, climate change and sea level rise; global trends in consumer/industry preferences of farm commodities.

This will also monitor trade and collect market intelligence with respect to GM crops and products and follow the trend of organic markets and watch international developments to identify niche markets, monitor countries that are rejecting GM foods and feed this intelligence to concerned agencies. Priorities for crops and traits should be set after conducting a need assessment exercise in various farming zones. However, an indicative list has been suggested by MS Swaminathan Task Force.

— *Crop:* Priority target traits in crop plants would be yield increase, pest and disease resistance, abiotic stress tolerance, enhanced quality, and shelf life, engineering male sterility and development of apomixis. Crops of priority should be rice, wheat, maize, sorghum, pigeon pea, chickpea, moong bean, groundnut, mustard, soybean, cotton, sugarcane, potato, tomato, cole crops, banana, papayas and citrus. In priority crops equal emphasis should be given to GM hybrids and new varieties. The varieties in contrast to hybrids, are preferred by small farmers as they can use their own farm saved seeds for at least three or four years. In case of hybrids, research on the introduction of genetic factors for apomixis would be supported so that resource-poor farmers can derive benefits from hybrid vigour without having to buy expensive seeds every cropping season.

— *Livestock:* Priority target traits in livestock would be enhanced fertility and reproductive performance, improved quality, resistance to diseases for reduced drug use, production of therapeutically useful products and quality feed. Livestock of priority would be buffalo, cattle, sheep and goat. Emphasis would be given to animal healthcare, nutrition, development of transgenics and genomics. It is proposed to set up an autonomous institution for animal biotechnology.

— *Aquaculture and marine biotechnology:* Application of biotechnology would be crucial in disease resistance, enhanced productivity, fertility and reproductive growth, use of aquatic species as bioreactors for production of industrial products, value added products from sea weeds and other marine taxa and biosensors for pollution monitoring. Species of priority in fisheries would be carps, tiger shrimps and fresh water prawns. It is proposed to set up under the auspices of DBT and autonomous centre for marine biotechnology

— *Food and nutrition:* R&D would be focused on: development of biotechnology tools for evaluating food safety, development of rapid diagnostic kits for detection of various food borne pathogens; development of analogical methods for detection of genetically modified foods and products derived there from; development of nutraceuticals / health food supplements/ functional foods for holistic health; development of pre-cooked, ready-to-eat, nutritionally fortified food for school going children; development of suitable pro-biotics for therapeutic purposes and development of bio food additives. It is proposed to set up (under the auspices of Department of Biotechnology) an autonomous institute for nutritional biology and food biotechnology (2006).

— *Biofertilizers and biopesticides:* Priorities would include screening of elite strains of micros-organisms and / or productions of super-strains, better understanding of the dynamics of symbiotic nitrogen fixation, process optimization for fermentor - based technologies, improved shelf life, better quality standards, setting up accredited quality control laboratories and standardization of GMP guidelines. Integrated nutrient management system would be further strengthened.

Bioresources

The combined annual global market for the products derived from bioresources is roughly between US$ 500 billion and US$ 800 billion. India is one of the 12 global mega biodiversity centres harbouring approximately 8% of the global biodiversity existing in only 2.4% of the land area. The country is also home to two of the world's 25 hotspots. The varied cultural diversity across the country as well as a very ancient traditional knowledge system associated with the biodiversity represents added assets. Nonetheless, much of this biodiversity is in peril owing, in the main, to anthropogenic causes.

Thus, if the goal of converting our bioresources - animal, plant, microbial and marine - into commercially useful products and processes is to be realized, we need to not only conserve the biodiversity and but also utilize it in a sustainable manner. Absence of a good quantitative information network on bioresources combining remote-sensing data and ground surveys is a major constraint. The situation is even worse for microorganisms. Field- and marine biologists rarely work with molecular scientists and chemists, pharmacologists or other experts, and there is practically no bioprospecting industry. While our traditional knowledge base would be the starting for bioprospecting, ethics and equity should be our guiding principles in benefit sharing.

Animal Resources

India is home to an estimated 86,874 species of animals accounting for 7.25% of global animal diversity. The degree of endemism is high and populations of several animal groups are diminishing due to habitat destruction and poaching. Several species, their products and the services rendered by them are crucial to our economic well-being: pollination services by insects to our agricultural and forestry crops, honey, silk, lac, musk, skins are just a few examples. Other species (e.g., molluscs, frogs, toads, spiders, termites, and snakes) represent potential reservoirs of useful products such as toxins, venoms, enzymes, therapeutic molecules and other bioactive substances.

Prospecting for these and other products should be a priority. Biotechnology should be effectively employed for molecular characterization along with bioscreens in search of useful products. Utilization of selected species as bioreactors for production of complex proteins is another important opportunity.

Plant Resources

India has a huge treasure of plant resources with over 45,000 known species representing 11% of earth's flora. In terms of flowering plant diversity alone, India ranks tenth in the world. About 33% of flowering plants and 29% of total plants are endemic to the country. Genetic erosion is rampant and conservation is a priority. Prospecting of wild plant resources using molecular approaches and mechanism-based screening should be used to identify novel genes (temperature, drought, salinity tolerant) and gene products (therapeutic compounds, dyes, essential oils, biocontrol agents, gums resins and taxmins).

There are potential ornamentals, including foliage - and flower - bearing plants that could be bulked up to be subsequently cultivated on large scale for domestic and international trade. Bioconversion - both cellular and microbial -should be employed to convert intermediates of secondary metabolism into valued added products. Application of genomics, proteomics and metabolomics in carefully selected plants will be very useful.

Biotechnology can contribute substantially in providing cost-effective therapeutically active biomolecules through target/mechanism - based screens, biotransformation, metabolic engineering and transgenic approaches. Biotechnology should also be utilized to add value to our traditional knowledge especially Ayurveda, Sidha and Unani systems as well as tribal and folk medicine. Medicinal plants are also the prime targets of bioprospecting. Besides, the tools of biotechnology can be used for conservation and characterization of plants. Fossil fuels are chief contributors to urban air pollution and a major source of greenhouse gases (GHGs) - considered to be the main causes behind the climate change phenomena.

In contrast, biofuels are renewable; hence, they can supplement hydrocarbon fuels, assist in their conservation, as well as mitigate their adverse effects on the climate. Two major biofuels for the transport sector, bioethanol and biodiesel, are fast becoming popular in many countries around the world. While bio-ethanol (called ethanol) is produced from raw materials such as molasses, beet, sugarcane juice, grains and tubers, biodiesel is produced from oil (derived from oil-bearing seeds such as Jatropha curcas, Pongamia pinnata i.e.karanja).

India imports nearly 70% of its annual crude petroleum requirement. The net oil import bill (import minus exports) was Rs 77,058 crore (Rs 770.58 billion) in 2003-04 as against Rs 74,174 crore (Rs 741.74 billion) the previous year. This expenditure on crude purchase impacts the country's foreign exchange reserves in a big way. The petroleum industry now looks very committed to the use of ethanol as fuel. It is estimated that 75% of the increase in world demand for oil will come from transport. India's transport sector will consume ever-higher amounts of fuel over the coming years. Being one of the largest producers of agro products, including sugarcane, India should take a lead in this worldwide effort at promoting sustainable development.

Microbial Resources

Currently only five percent microbes are culturable but there are others of considerable potential value that need to be characterized by new and novel techniques. The five percent culturable microbes have been a source of valuable products. India should play a leading role in the study and utilization of microbial resources. Our priorities include: preparation of inventories based on primary and secondary data; exploration of micro flora in the north-eastern region of the country, and extreme habitats for discovery of novel bioactive molecules; and study, characterization and screening of uncultivable microbes through appropriate molecular approaches.

Marine Resources

The economic zone of the sea as a source of novel genes and gene products - biopolymers, novel enzymes, new therapeutic leads, and other value-added products such as osmo-tolerant crops - has hardly been explored. Marine organisms also present immense potential as biosensors for pollution monitoring as well as bioreactors for production of novel products. Besides, the study of deep-sea organisms including marine microbes has tremendous implications for human health. Expertise in these diverse areas is scattered across a number of agencies/institutions. Strategic Actions would be in the following areas.

Strategic Actions are as follows:

— There is an acute shortage of expertise in India particularly in taxonomy (the science of the classification of the living and extinct organisms) and microbial ecology. We need to take urgent steps to rectify this.

— Support to capacity building in microbial taxonomy through intensive training programmes at graduate and post-graduate levels

— Promotion of horizontal networking between remote sensing experts, field biologists and computer specialists for inventorisation of bioresources based both on primary and secondary sources of information

— Promotion of closer and effective interaction between biotechnologists, foresters, oceanographers and field biologists.

— Ensure that the use of bioresources be sustainable by regulating the harvesting of medicinal plants

— Formulate a policy to regulate the procurement and sale of medicinal plants in India. Introduce regulatory norms prescribed by DCGI that evaluate the efficacy, safety, and quality of herbal products, which currently are exempt from the scope of any regulation of the DCGI.

— Establish a close working relationship between field scientists, pharmacologists and clinicians so that an all round integration is achieved.

— Public-private partnerships need be promoted for product generation

— Creation of a gene bank for maintaining 'mined' genes

— There is, as on date, only one international depository authority (IDA) in the country at the Microbial Type Culture Collection (MTCC) at IMTECH, Chandigarh; however, for securing our IPR interests, we need to initiate steps to establish a few more centres as IDAs.

— Currently, MTCC does not accept biological materials such as cell lines, cyanobacteria, viruses etc. as it has no expertise or facilities for this purpose. Yet, these are essential for filing patents. IDAs in other countries may refuse to accept such material as they may be potentially hazardous or the shipments may have restrictions. In view of this, the scope of MTCC needs to be expanded by upgrading the existing expertise and infrastructure. Alternately, IDAs should be set up where such expertise and infrastructure are available.

— End products from bioprospecting need to be tested for a variety of parameters before commercial production can begin. There is a need to set up appropriate facilities for such late stage testing of products.

— An autonomous Centre for Marine Biotechnology is proposed to be set up under the auspices of DBT

— An autonomous Institute for Biotechnology for Herbal Medicine under the auspices of DBT is proposed to be established.

Environment

Environmental issues concern everyone. Biotechnology has tremendous potential for application to a wide variety of environmental issues including conservation and characterization of rare or endangered taxa, afforestation and reforestation. It can help in rapid monitoring of environmental pollution, ecorestoration of degraded sites such as mining spoil dumps, treatment of effluents discharged by industries (oil refineries, dyeing and textile units, paper and pulp mills, tanneries, pesticide units etc.), treatment of solid waste, and so on. A number of technologies have already been generated and demonstrated in the country. The real challenge is their adoption by the industry, which has been somewhat uneven.

In general, corporate groups have not been overly enthusiastic in adopting biotechnologies even where they have proven efficacy. The reasons may be several: industry is usually not involved at the planning stage of experiment; enforcement of environmental laws is not always strict or uniform at the ground level and offenders can often escape with impunity; manufacturers frequently change their production schedules based on demand profiles resulting in varied streams of effluents, but microbial consortia specifically designed to one set of effluents may be ineffective in breaking down the changed pollutants.

The goal of environmental biotechnology would be to provide cost-effective and clean alternatives for risk assessment and quality monitoring, eco-restoration of degraded habitats, conversion of toxic recalcitrant chemicals into harmless byproducts, bioremediation of wastes, value-added products from biomass, control of biological invasion through biotechnological interventions, greener process technologies, and effective ex situ conservation strategies. These can be fulfilled through a deeper understanding - and engineering - of the metabolic pathways for degradation of toxicants, environmental genomics and proteomics, and other molecular techniques. Strategic Actions are as follows:

For the diffusion of biotechnologies to be successful the following measures should be put in place:

— Ensuring effective and closer horizontal linkages between research workers and the user corporate groups

— Public-private partnership in research and application of clean technologies

— Strict enforcement of the 'polluter pays' principle. This would require interaction with law enforcement agencies

— Capacity building and training, through workshops, of law enforcement officials, municipal workers, state government functionaries and corporate groups on role and relevance of biotechnology in waste treatment

— Steps to encourage small and medium business companies in producing eco-friendly products, microbial consortia etc. for wider usage

— Building greater awareness for protection of proprietary rights of microbial consortia through appropriate methods

Greater inter-agency coordination between DBT, MoEF, ICAR, CSIR, CPCB, user agencies and industry through an inter-ministerial Task Force.

Industrial Biotechnology

At present, a third wave of biotechnology - industrial biotechnology - is strongly developing. Industrial biotechnology (also referred to as white biotechnology) uses biological systems for the production of useful chemical entities. This technology is mainly based on biocatalysis and fermentation technology in combination with recent breakthroughs in the forefront of molecular genetics and metabolic engineering. This new technology has developed into a main contributor to the so-called green chemistry, in which renewable resources such as sugars or vegetable oils are converted into a wide variety of chemical substances such as fine and bulk chemicals, pharmaceuticals, bio-colorants, solvents, bio-plastics, vitamins, food additives, bio-pesticides and bio-fuels such as bio-ethanol and bio-diesel.

The application of industrial biotechnology offers significant ecological advantages. Agricultural crops are used starting raw materials, instead of using fossil resources such as crude oil and gas. This technology consequently has a beneficial effect on greenhouse gas emissions and at the same time supports the agricultural sector producing these raw materials. Industrial biotechnology frequently shows significant performance benefits compared to conventional chemical technology.

Strategic Actions are as follows:

— Focus in industrial biotechnology will be on reducing chemical and toxic load in our effluent streams, developing non-fossil fuels that are ecofriendly and developing green technologies in Industrial processing.

— Encourage public-private partnership to promote investment in this sector.

— Promotion of industrial biotechnology in strategic areas of manufacturing and developing green technologies.

Preventive and Therapeutic Medical Biotechnology

A healthy population is essential for economic development. Important contributors to the total disease burden are infections like HIV-AIDS, tuberculosis, malaria, respiratory infections and chronic diseases affecting the heart and blood vessels, neuro-psychiatric disorders, diabetes and cancer. It is important to synchronize the technology and products with the local needs of the health system and to facilitate technology diffusion into health practice. Increasing knowledge about pathogen genomes and subtypes, host responses to infectious challenges, molecular determinants of virulence and protective immunity and novel understanding mechanisms underlying escaped immunity and ways to develop novel immunogens will guide development of vaccines against infectious diseases.

Translational research and ability to rapidly evaluate multiple candidates in clinical trials can help accelerate the pace of vaccine development. New directions in manufacturing and delivery are emerging. Major opportunities to control costs are the more efficient processes for manufacturing of new pharmaceuticals, more efficient systems for production of therapeutic proteins and biomaterials and development of drug delivery systems that release drugs at a target site.

A shift from parenteral to oral or transcutaneous administration of drugs and vaccine holds the promise of simplifying delivery in health systems. Medical biotechnology offers a significant possibility for Indian industry to establish a strong pharmacy sector, a growing number of small and medium biotechnology companies, a large network of universities, research institutes, and medical schools and low cost of product evaluation. The medical biotechnology sector annually contributes over

2/3rd of the biotechnology industry turnover. The Indian vaccine industry has highlighted India's potential by emerging as an important source of low cost vaccine for the entire developing world.

Further, economic opportunities through contract research and manufacturing through global partnerships are large if supported by enabling government policies and incentives. The policy goal is to accord high priority to basic and applied research, to strengthen capacity in pre-clinical and clinical product evaluation technologies relevant to all aspects of health and medical care-predictive, preventive, therapeutic and restorative will be supported. Innovation will be supported through new granting mechanisms to support interdisciplinary networks and public private partnerships. Strategic Actions are as follows:

Research emphasis

— Basic and applied research would be supported in molecular and cellular biology, genomics, proteomics, system biology, stem cell biology, RNA interference, host response and new platform technologies.

— Pathogenesis of major diseases and molecular mechanics of disease transmission would be investigated

— Product development will be focused on vaccines, diagnostics, new therapies based on cell and tissue replacement, therapeutic antibodies, herbal medicine, plant based medicine, nucleic acids, therapeutics, drug and vaccine delivery systems, new anti microbial agents

— Research to improve production and manufacturing process and local production of biological reagents for development of diagnostics will be supported.

Improvements in infrastructure and networks

— A centre for translational research will be established. This new institute will be interdisciplinary and will deal with technology policy for public health, molecular pathogenesis of disease, technology development, scale up, product evaluation and technology diffusion into programmes. Centre will be unique in having a pool of scientists, physicians, engineers, and public health persons working on public health grand challenges. This institute will work through public-private partnerships and be a training centre for product development, IPR and regulation.

— A mission mode programme will be initiated in biomaterial and medical device area as an integrated effort by the Department of Science & Technology and Department of Biotechnology. The goal is to promote R&D and industrial activity.

— Two centres of molecular medicine will be supported within medical school system closely interacting with basic science institutes.

— A virtual network of stem cell centres will be established, using a city cluster approach to network scientists and clinicians. Two core stem cell research centres will be established together with several network subclusters. An umbilical cord stem cell bank will be established.

— Mechanism based screening of herbal drugs known in traditional Indian systems would be carried out so as to get value added therapeutics products quickly

— An inter agency task force of ICMR, Department of Biotechnology, and DST will be established to suggest strategies for strengthening medical school based research. Capacity related to translational biology, clinical trials, molecular epidemiology and product development would be strengthened. Integrated MD-PhD programs will be supported.

Streamline guidelines and procedures for the approval of recombinant pharmaceutical products: Currently there are multiple regulators, multiple ministries, lack of coordination between these regulators, Over-lapping and duplication of responsibilities of these regulators, lack of a linear progression in the approval process and committees working outside their area of expertise. A new procedural framework for Biopharmaceuticals, which has streamlined the regulatory process:

— IBSC will monitor all development work (upto 20 Litres) and recommend to RCGM for Animal Toxicity Tests (ATT) & Scale up.

— RCGM will evaluate the recombinant technology & grant permission for scale up - R & D, review and approve for preclinical animal toxicity tests and evaluate ATT data & recommend to DCGI for Human Clinical Trial (HCT).

— DCGI will permit Human Clinical Trials, review Human Clinical Trial Data, grant permission for Manufacture and Marketing the product and inspect the facility where product is manufactured.

— GEAC will review the manufacturing process to ensure that the LMO (living modified organism) is "inactivated" during the process and send its recommendations to the Drugs Controller General of India within the specified time. The GEAC would confine its approval role to LMOs and Category 3 and 4 microorganisms.

Regenerative and Genomic Medicine

The first wave of real healthy life extension therapies seems likely to result from research stem cells and regenerative medicine which helps natural healing processes to work faster, or uses special materials to regrow missing or damaged tissue. Doctors use regenerative medicine to speed up healing, and to help heal injuries that cannot heal on their own. Regenerative therapies have been demonstrated (in trials or the laboratory) to heal broken bones, bad burns, blindness, deafness, heart damage, nerve damage, Parkinson's and other conditions. Regenerative medicine will result in extended healthy lifespan; we will be able to repair some of the damage caused by aging, organ by organ. The first crop of simple stem cell therapies for regenerative medicine might be only a few years away from widespread availability.

There are major scientific and ethical challenges and safety concerns that must be overcome in taking stem cell based technology for bench to bedside. As it is rapidly evolving field, the existing national (ICMR) guidelines need to be updated and supported by clear articulated procedures. India must consider the potential medical applications of stem cell research. We must reassure end users on the safety and quality by ensuring regulation on stem lines having stable characterizations so that safety risks are predictable. We must reassure suppliers by regulation from lab to market.

Strategic Actions are as follows:

— Formulate a comprehensive Human Tissue Act (end 2005) with codes and guidance for regenerative medicine. In the intension, ICMR and DBT will support existing guidelines for stem cell research with clear procedures to be followed by scientists and physician.

— DNA and stem cell banking facilities will be created.

— Lay down clearer laws on animal testing in the country for progress to be made in this sector.

— Emphasize on Intellectual Property Rights, confidentiality and feedback

— Regulation for human tissue engineered products.

— Public awareness to be created in order to allay fears through education programmes, industry conferences and seminars.

Diagnostics for Emerging Medical Paradigm

There is potential to generate a new repertoire of tools for screening people for risk of disease, for early detection of infections and chronic diseases and for predicting outcome. In certain circumstances, single tests are requires to detect multiple pathogens or biochemical abnormalities. To be widely useful, diagnostics need to be real time and low cost. Advances in biosensors and gene amplification are in the offing to enable real time medicine. Immuno proteomics has the potential to reveal multiple targets for development of diagnostics for diseases for which existing tools are unsatisfactory.

For chronic diseases, a shift from treating disease on an individual basis is visualized by genetic assessment of likelihood of benefit from a therapeutic intervention, the so-called personalized medicine. It is seen that most drugs work in only a proportion of patients, targeting therapy to the right sub-group will not only make therapy more efficacious but also make evaluation of newer products cheaper. Pharmacogenomics is a rapidly growing segment that provides a wealth of information pertaining to defective or missing genes, which call for differentiated medicine - a new avenue for drug research. This emerging discipline combines both infotech and biotech skills in augmenting high-speed data mining of both genotypic and phenotypic information with a view to evolving new forms of medical diagnostics and therapies.

Gene regulation and other bio-algorithms will form the core of a new wave of diagnostics that are now being referred to as 'theranostics'. India can be positioned as the hub for differentiated medicine as the country offers one of the most affordable development bases for personalized medicines. Personalized therapies will demand extensive clinical data generated from well-differentiated patient populations. India has one of the most desired disease and patient profiles that can enable such studies. Coupled with this is the need for a large number of novel diagnostics based on gene and non-gene based platforms. These are clearly large opportunities for Indian Biotech companies to pursue.

Personalized drugs also address the affordability factor for expensive therapies such as those that are involved with cancer. Some important barriers to improving the clinical utility of such knowledge exist. These include the highly complex nature of the problem, little incentive for industry to move to genomic-based approach, and lack of provider education.

Strategic Actions are as follows:

— Establish a cell for Diagnostic Biotechnology to encourage and support studies into the clinical application of pharmacogenomics. This cell should be well positioned to overcome barriers in its work to bring pharmacogenomics to the clinical setting.

— Encourage research-involving investigators with both clinical practice and pharmacology / pharmacokinetics expertise while at the same time keeping the overall goal of clinical application / utility in focus.

— Provide incentives for this group of clinician-researchers to bring these scientific advances to the patient bedside

— Support education programs to providers of the importance of this field and its utility.

— Encourage biopharmaceutical companies to include pharmacogenomic data in their drug submissions

Bio-engineering and Nano Biotechnology

Bioengineering covers a wide range of areas such as tissue engineering, biomaterials for therapeutics, biomedical devices and instrumentation, biomedical sensors etc. Tissue engineering, especially of tissues derived from the patient's own cells, offers total acceptance and integration, unlike non-living materials or tissues from other species. Research is focused on developing non-immunogenic materials to serve as scaffolds for regeneration of damaged tissue. Bone and cartilage can be grown today and there is potential for other tissue. Developments in novel biomaterials for micro-particle and nano-particle encapsulated drugs, proteins and other molecules have offered improvement in quality of many therapies with minimal side effects.

Bioengineering offers opportunities for indigenous development of critical implants and extra corporeal devices. Nanoscale structured materials and devices hold a great promise for advanced diagnostics, biosensors, targeted delivery and smart drugs. The application of nanotechnology in bioengineering together with biotechnology offers a great new range of advanced biomaterials with enhanced functionality; and intertwined with tissue engineering, it has the potential to provide true organ replacement technology of the coming decade. While recognizing this potential, it is important to assess not only the efficacy, but also safety of these new interventions regard to human health.

The current market for medicinal devices such as implantables, disposables wound care, dental and orthopaedic materials etc is estimated at around Rs 7000 crores another Rs 5000 crores for the medical instrumentation sector in the country, with a growth rate of 15% per year. Nearly 80% of this demand is met by imports. Major factors limiting the growth of indigenous medical devices industry are the high cost and non-availability of imported technology, higher risks involved in producing and marketing medical devices, inadequate indigenous technology development and production of biomaterials and device and lack of a regulatory authority for medical devices in the country. Strategic Actions are as follows:

In bioengineering research emphasis will be on:

— Development of tissue engineered skin, cartilage, cornea, acute liver support, large segment bone repair and small diameter artery

— Biomaterials for drug delivery and controlled release

— Regenerative therapy for the failing myocardium through LVAD support, drug therapy and stem cell technology

— Advanced blood compatible surface fir cardiovascular devices

— Advanced burn and wound dressings

— Bioinstrumentation and physiologic monitoring

— Biosensors for detecting and monitoring metabolites and identifying specific genetic materials and for home monitoring of critical parameters like creatinine, cholesterol and triglycerides

— Dental and orthopaedic materials based on polymer-ceramic composites

— Test methods for safety evaluation of tissue engineered and combinational products.

Pre-eminent applications derived from Nano-biotechnology include drug delivery systems and diagnostics. R&D support will be focused on:

— Micro-electro-mechanical systems (MEMS), medical electronics and

— optics

— Bio-molecular chips for analysis

— Carbon nanotube based biosensors

— DNA nanowire and electrical characterization of DNA

Establishing effective institutional mechanisms

— An inter agency working group will be formed to develop a common vision and working strategy in this area

— Appropriate regulatory process will be established to hasten introduction of new medical devices through inter-ministerial consultation

— Focused multi-disciplinary research groups shall be formed with clear mandates, targets and adequate funding; these will be monitored regularly for accountability on research output.

— Suitable institution-industry linkage will be built for technology proving and scaling up of products / medical devices developed at laboratory level

Bio-informatics and IT

Bioinformatics has proved to be a powerful tool for advanced research and development in the field of biotechnology. Bioinformatics holds out strong expectations of reducing the cost and time of development of new products such as new drugs and vaccines, plants with specific properties and resistance to pests and diseases, new protein molecules and biological materials and properties. As the full genome sequences, data from micros arrays, proteomics as well as species data at the taxonomic level became available, integration of these databases require sophisticated bioinformatics tools.

Organizing these data into suitable databases and developing appropriate software tools for analyzing the same are going to be major challenges. India has the potential to develop such resources at an affordable cost. Bioinformatics in India can be used effectively for promoting research in biology; prospecting; conservation and management of bioresources; evaluation of products, processes and raw materials, managing complex data required to plan and monitor major national programs; and meeting the growing need of contract services and business outsourcing in pharma and biotechnology sectors.

One of the major challenges in optimum exploitation of bioinformatics for solving life science issues is the formulation of appropriate computational biology problems that can be addressed through IT tools. This requires adequate appreciation of the scope and strength of bioinformatics by the biologists and basic understanding of the biological sciences by the information scientists. The solution lies in having adequate leaders with expertise in both life sciences and information technology and strong institutional / program tie-up between specialists from both the fields.

In India, Informatics for life Sciences is an emerging sector - the market size is still quite limited (many verticals each of size USD 20 million - USD 100 million). India has strengths in Chemistry and Computer Science, Software, Health Care and biology. An extensive bioinformatics network has been established covering more than 60 centres spread all over the country. The network has generated human resources through education and training programs at different levels. Some of them have the potential of emerging as advanced R&D facilities.

To promote R&D and to utilize the business opportunities would require creation of broadband connectivity, high performance computing facilities, virtual reality centres, availability of high quality trained manpower, interactions with bioinformatics centres in different countries and industry academia interactions for joint database and software creation. Strategic actions are as follows:

Human resource development

— A continuous talent pipeline will be ensured by producing 50-100 quality PhDs, 500 M.Sc and 500 advanced diploma holders in bioinformatics every year

— A national testing program will be put in place for accreditation of students at different levels

— The fellowships of PhD students shall be increased

— Industrial training will be introduced for students pursuing advanced diploma course in bioinformatics

— Virtual classrooms will be established in identified institutions. Teaching material in electronic form will be developed and made available at a reasonable cost.

— Industry participation in developing course content and materials will be ensured.

Infrastructure development

— Super computing facilities with 10 teraflops computing capacity will be created on biogrid to promote protein folding and drug design activities

— Broadband internet connectivity shall be provided for bioinformatics research and manpower development at subsidized rates

Testing of public domain resources

— Institutional mechanism will be put in place for testing public domain databases and software and making them available to the users from the academia and the industry. After such testing, these databases and algorithms will be graded so that scientists can use them with higher confidence.

— Commercial databases and software will be tested before the industry invests in the products. Such service will help the industry to reduce their costs and use only certified products

Inter agency coordination

— There are many government departments and agencies, which are supporting bioinformatics activities. These include CSIR, ICMR, ICAR, DST and MIT. An independent inter departmental agency will be established to coordinate these activities among these departments and agencies.

— The agency will be empowered by legislation to provide the direction and oversee the implementation of the coordinated action plan.

Strengthening of DICs and sub DICs

— The CoEs DICs and sub DICs of BTISnet will be strengthened for hardcore research in bioinformatics as well as high-end human resource development.

— Department of Biotechnology will increase the investment in this sector three times over a period of five years

Bio IT parks and promotion of bioinformatics industries

— Department of Biotechnology in association with the Ministry of IT will set up bio IT parks for the promotion of the bioinformatics industry.

— High-risk projects in bioinformatics will be promoted through special support mechanism including public-private partnerships.

Clinical Biotechnology

The cost of launching a new drug into the marked is estimated to cost between $300-500 million of which the cost split between Research and Development is 25% : 75% which would translate to an approximate cost of US$200-400 million for patient clinical studies and trials which form the main components of drug development. The potential of being a key player in this segment is high and remunerative. India has made tremendous progress in clinical biotechnology over the past few years.

However, the infrastructure required to identify, document and monitor patients under clinical trials need to be first put in place before India can partake in this activity. There is also an exciting opportunity of conducting longitudinal studies in disease segments for prospecting new biomarkers and novel pharmacogenomic information both yielding high value Intellectual Property.

With the global pharmaceuticals companies looking outward to reduce their ballooning research costs, a country like India is in a good position to tap the new business opportunities. Due to the emphasis on outsourcing in the nearly stagnant economies to cut costs and retain competitiveness, India is being considered as a destination for contract research in the pharma sector. Custom research is a services model that most Indian biotech companies have opted for at their start-up stage in order to earn early revenues with which to fund infrastructure and scientist salaries. These companies harbour ambitions of original R&D once they reach a certain profit level.

Since research service is about delivery of results, the Government has an important role to play in facilitating the industry. India needs to be promoted as a research service destination. The IP environment is confusing since there is no mechanism or standard for contract sharing. The industry needs to collaborate with the academia and a code of conduct for biotech members has to be designed. Number of clinical trials that Indian companies would be conducting will increase tremendously for products developed indigenously and imported. Measures are needed that ensure patent safety and compliance with ethical and regulatory requirements.

The quality of trials should be such that data generated are accepted globally. Clarity in rules is required related to biotech drugs developed by Indian companies abroad, drugs discovered abroad and licensed to an Indian company, and drugs discovered by an Indian subsidiary of foreign company. The policy goal would be to promote consultations among all stakeholders within the Government and private sector to evolve clear guidelines and procedures.

Strategic Actions are as follows:

— Frame appropriate rules and procedures to support contract research services through stakeholder consultation.

— Harmonise and streamline the regulatory issues for important and export of biological materials.

— Review eligibility of virtual export of R&D services through contract research for fiscal incentives.

— Address the operational deficiencies through stakeholder consultations for conducting clinical trials.

— Develop a Good Clinical Trial Practice Manual taking into account international guidelines and disseminate these widely.

— Promote, train and support clinical trial investigators as a collaborative ICMR, DBT initiative.

— Strengthen clinical trial capacity in medical schools and hospitals and create centres of excellence.

— Address issues and frame guidelines for patent protection including issue of liability.

— Strengthen institutional ethics committees to bring them at par with global benchmark.

Intellectual Property and Patent Law

The development of capabilities for the effective management of Intellectual Property (IP) is an important element in securing the benefits of public and private sector research in biotechnology. Filings of patents both in India and aboard are critical to the growth of the Indian biotech Sector. The expenses for filing patents especially outside India are prohibitive and a major barrier to effective Intellectual Property Management within the country. Whilst expenses incurred with respect to filing of patents in India is eligible for weighted deduction, similar benefit is not provided for expenses incurred with regard to filing patents outside India.

As Intellectual Property Right (IPR)* creation is a pre-requisite for exports to the regulated markets, it is recommended that expenditure incurred with regard to filing patents outside India be also eligible for weighted deduction U/S 35 (2AB). This is also imperative in the new WTO-TRIPS regime, which has taken effect on 1st January 2005.

Strategic Actions are as follows: Administration of the new intellectual property rights regime should be improved. This will be achieved by

— Encouraging science graduates to pursue law for better understanding of IPR related issues

— Inclusion of IPR related issues in curriculum of law colleges for facilitating filing of international patents, license negotiation, dispute resolution etc.

— Training scientists and technology transfer professionals in the strategy of intellectual property protection relating to assessment of patentability, prior art examination and technology transfer issues;

— Training patent attorneys on science subject(s) and improving mechanisms for IPR administration through reforms and creation of patent offices, patent codes and ensuring adequate availability of patent attorneys. This will be promoted to an effective inter-ministerial collaboration.

— Setting up of an arbitration council to redress IPR disputes The setting up of an arbitration council will help in improving the perception and increasing International confidence towards IPR protection in India.

— A Rs 50 crore budget be allocated to substantially improve the current Patent infrastructure and set up additional offices in cities such as Bangalore & Hyderabad.

— The Department of Biotechnology will engage in constant dialogue with the Government of India and WTO-TRIPS to address patentability issues in Biotechnology and their future inclusion in the Patents Bill through ammendments.

Bibliography

Batten, T. R., *Communities and their Development. An introductory study with special reference to the Tropics*, London: Oxford University Press. 1957

_______________. and Batten M. *The Non-Directive Approach in Group and Community Work*, London: Oxford University Press, 1967

Broady, M., Clarke, R., Marks, H., Mills, R., Sims, E., Smith, M. & White, L. (ed. Clarke, R.), "Enterprising Neighbours". *The development of the community association in Britain, London: National Federation of Community Organisations*, 1990

Cannan, C., Berry, L. and Lyons, K., *Social Work and Europe*, London: Macmillan, 1992.

Craig, G., Mayo, M. and Sharman, N. (eds.), "Jobs and Community Action". *Community Work* 5, London: Routledge and Kegan Paul, 1979.

_______________, Derricourt, N. and Loney, M. (eds.), "Community Work and the State". *Towards a radical practice. Community Work* 8, London: Routledge and Kegan Paul, 1982.

Curno, P. (ed.) "Political Issues and Community Work". *Community Work* 4, London: Routledge and Kegan Paul, 1978.

Francis, D., Henderson, P. and Thomas, D. N., *A Survey of Community Workers in the United Kingdom. National Institute for Social Work*. 1984.

Mayo, M. (ed.), "Women in the Community". *Community Work* 3, London: Routledge and Kegan Paul, 1977.

Ohri, A., Manning, B. and Curno, P. (eds.), "Community Work and Racism". *Community Work* 7, London: Routledge and Kegan Paul, 1982.

Smith, L. and Jones, D. (eds.), "Deprivation, Participation and Community Action". *Community Work* 6, London: Routledge and Kegan Paul, 1981.

Index